Teach Me
to Love Myself

Teach Me to Love Myself

Memoir of a Pioneering Deaf Therapist

Holly Elliott

Teach Me to Love Myself
Holly Elliott

Copyright© 2008 by Holly Elliott

cover and interior design by White River Press

White River Press
PO Box 4624
White River Junction, VT 05001

Library of Congress Cataloging-in-Publication

Elliott, Holly, 1920-2002.
  Teach me to love myself : memoir of a deafened
counselor/therapist / Holly Elliott.
      p. ; cm.
  ISBN 978-1-935052-08-1 (pbk. : alk. paper)
  1. Elliott, Holly, 1920-2002. 2. Deaf--United States--
Biography. 3. Counselors--United States--Biography. 4.
Psychotherapists--United States--Biography. I. Title.
  [DNLM: 1. Counselors--Personal Narratives. 2. Deafness--
Personal Narratives. 3. Cochlear Implants--Personal Narratives.
4. Professional-Patient Relations--Personal Narratives. WZ
100 E46t 2008]
  HV2534.E45 2008
  616.89'14092--dc22
  [B]
                                        2008035535

DEDICATION

To Laurel Glass: In Memoriam
With gratitude for her compassion, wisdom, and friendship.

ACKNOWLEDGMENTS

Chapter X, "How to Succeed in College without Really Hearing," first appeared in *The Volta Review*, Vol. 72, No. 2 (March 1970), 157–60, and is used here with permission.

The poem "Culture Shock upon a Rooftop in Monaco" was originally published in *Deaf American Monograph* (1994) and reprinted in *Signs of Solidarity: Ministries with People Who are Deaf, Late-Deafened, Hard of Hearing and Deaf-Blind* (Second Edition: National Committee on Ministries with Deaf, Late-Deafened, Hard of Hearing and Deaf-Blind People and the Health and Welfare Ministries Unit of the General Board of Global Ministries of the United Methodist Church, 2003).

TABLE OF CONTENTS

I.   Teach Me to Love Myself (1973)   11

II.   What Script?   19

III. Who Says I'm Deaf?   25

IV.   Was It Enough?   33

V.   A Necessary Turning Point   45

VI.   I Want to Go Home and Bake a Good Cheesecake   49

VII. "When I Am Dead Sing No Sad Songs for Me"   55

VIII. Suicide or Crucifixion?   63

IX.   Don't Be Close   67

X.   How to Succeed in College Without
      Really Hearing   73

XI.   In the Real Essence of Life We Are Alone   77

XII. Therapist–Status–Not–Coded   81

XIII. Total Communication   85

XIV.   Try Listening to Rock When All You Can Hear
       Is the Bass   95

XV.   The Silent Message   101

XVI.   Man Also Needs to Attain His Goals   111

XVII.   I'm Doing It My Way Now   113

XVIII. September 1998   117

Final Words   121

Biographical Note   123

one

Teach Me to Love Myself (1973)

Mary was distraught when she arrived for her appointment. Her anxiety level was high, causing her sign language to become a veritable blur, it flew so fast. I felt my own anxiety as I strained to understand the shapes: "Slow down, Mary! You're signing too fast for me!"

As Mary continued her story, part of my mind formed the content, but I was also conscious of the expressive feelings. Her face, really her whole body, reflected the moods signified by the continually changing configurations of her fingers, her hands, both independently and working together. Her hands dropped with her sad signs; her shoulders drooped, her face fell. Her happy signs were rare, but when she was telling about her children her hands moved upwards, her shoulders squared, and her face glowed. Occasionally she was angry; then her fingers clawed and jerked abruptly to a stop. Her body followed the lead of her hands in what seemed to be a sharp convulsive motion eloquently revealing the rage she felt.

A striking shift occurred when Mary felt defensive; her arms became a symbolic barrier, pushing the therapist away. I realized again how much more expressive than mere words sign language is. We often use words to hide our feelings, but the bodily accompaniments to sign could be much more revelatory. I knew if I could empathize with Mary's feelings, her signs would be more understandable.

Her shoulders drooped now. "Something wrong with me. Can't find love. I try and try, but can't find."

I had encountered this often with other deaf patients, this search for love. It had many manifestations, and occasionally in conjoint marriage counseling I felt that the walls must be bulging from the force of recriminations, though I knew that an audiometer would not register anything apart from whatever decibel count might be picked up from heavy breathing or an occasional stamped foot. At such times I could only regain control by intercepting the vision of the marital couple by intruding the "stop" sign between them. The edge of my right hand would hit forcibly on the palm of my left hand with enough angry intention in my own body to distract them from each other and focus their attention on me.

But that wasn't Mary's problem, and I opened her chart to review it before I replied. "How can you find love," I sighed to myself, "if you never really experienced love as a child?"

Mary and her second husband were both deaf (as was her first husband) and her children were hearing. Mary had been deaf from birth, the only deaf person in a rather large family. She told of a lonely childhood and recalled her stern father, her overprotective mother, and her ability to communicate with neither. Mary's mother, I realized, had probably seen overprotection as a form of love, but the message had been lost on Mary, who saw it only as restriction. At the age of six she had been shipped off to a distant residential school for the deaf where she had learned the language of sign. Her parents had never learned to sign and her communication with them had always been limited to natural gestures, as Mary had never been able to master lip-reading.

Poignantly she signed, "Teach me to love myself." I assured her that I could not teach her this, but I would very much like to help her do it herself.

"My friend told me goes to Deaf Clinic. She said you tell me I have to love myself before I can love another person."

Mary mentioned the name of her friend and I recalled seeing the woman the year before. I did not remember anything specific I had told the friend, but I supposed I told her that, for I certainly felt it was true. It's strange, I thought. We seldom know what particular statement will be picked up, enlarged upon, and passed on to a troubled friend. A beautiful statement, really. Wouldn't it be great if it was something that could be taught?

....

Mary's simple request jostled some insecurities in me that made me feel vaguely uncomfortable when she left. I was the only deaf therapist—and one of the newest—on the staff of an outpatient clinic that offers mental health services to deaf patients and their families. The services are similar to those in other community mental health centers, with important differences: the clinical staff has considerable experience in the specific problems of deafness, and can communicate in the language of signs. I thought of the patients I had seen, and how they reinforced the reading I had done to prepare for this new career. Deaf people probably have more than their share of emotional problems, I thought, although the vast majority lead happy and satisfying lives despite their communication barrier with hearing people. Many of my patients were under-educated and under-employed, but I recalled numerous studies indicating that deaf people are just as intelligent as hearing people, so underemployment is not necessarily due to a lack of native intelligence. Deaf people do not live in segregated areas, but often their social life is restricted by choice to the deaf community, and the so-called deaf cultures seem to cluster in areas near the state residential schools for the deaf.

And why not? I wondered. The same thing happens to the Spanish-speaking subculture, Asian subcultures, especially here on the Pacific coast. But there is an important difference. Most of the couples I've seen in marriage counseling were both deaf and almost without exception they had hearing children. Conversely, most of the deaf children I see in play therapy have hearing parents. Consequently, the deaf culture is even more complexly and inextricably intertwined with mainstream hearing culture than ethnic communities and families are with mainstream society. The shock of having deaf parents or deaf children is greater than language and customs. Yet many deaf—and those who work with them—often refer to the "deaf world" and the "hearing world" as if they were two separate entities. And, for many practical purposes, they are.

"I have been both hearing and deaf," I thought. "Are there really two worlds? Can I bridge them?"

Glancing down at my notes I saw that Mary and I had become deaf the same year: I at nineteen (though I struggled against the progressive hearing loss for years afterwards), Mary at birth. I had normal hearing and language development during my formative years; she did not. Until the age of about 45, I retained enough residual hearing to maintain the speech I had already learned; Mary never developed speech at all. But Mary had excellent language, which she expressed in signs that were far more fluent than mine, as I had only recently come to sign language. Yet she was quite willing to slow down her signs and finger spelling because she wanted to be understood, and she knew that I wanted to understand.

But I was frustrated that it was so difficult for me to acquire the ease and fluency in signs that Mary so beautifully conveyed. Was it age, the fact that it is harder to acquire a new language at midlife? Or was I blocked by unwillingness to be deaf? It is such a graceful language and can be used simultaneously with speech for greater clarity. Expressive body language enhances its manual beauty, facial expressions that mirror the soul. It quite literally reaches out to communicate.

I have been both hearing and deaf, I thought again.

....

Five years ago I decided to move from the hearing to the deaf world. The fact that I had fully admitted I was deaf, I felt, would be in my favor. But at a party I was introduced to a deaf man by another deaf man: "This is Holly. She is deaf, but she lives like a hearing person." Was he condescending or complimentary? Whatever he meant, his mild statement made me doubt that I could empathize with these vastly expressive and individually different people. My son Dennis recently wrote: "Isn't your situation unique in that you are both hearing and deaf?" But the received wisdom is that you're either hearing or deaf—you can't be both.

....

I recalled my European tour with a deaf group. I had decided to join the deaf world; buoyed by this decision, I decided to combine two experiences: I would see Europe for the first time and be deaf. It would be like a Berlitz course in sign language, which I was in the early stages of learning. It didn't work out that way. Concentrating on the deafness around me, I missed the humanity. Their signs were fast and difficult to follow. I spent a lot of time watching.

"Cultures meet reflectively upon a rooftop in Monaco—and clash," I wrote, turning to poetry to structure and control my feelings of alienation.

> I am deaf—not deaf.
> Hearing—not hearing.
> I talk to hearing, I am deaf.
> I talk to deaf and I am hearing.
> I talk to French, I am American.
> Part of all yet all of none.

I continued, reflecting on my sense of living on the periphery:

> I talk, I sign to Mariana.
> She does not comprehend my signs
> But writes and writes and studies French
> And takes the train alone to Nice.

One evening we walked to the Casino and found ourselves in a crowd, pressed against a fence. Barbara signed: "You ask them what they're waiting for. Please, you can talk."

"Pardon, Madam," I tapped a woman on the shoulder and pointed to the waiting crowd. "Pourquoi?"

"Elle est arrivée, la Princesse Grace!" And a great deal more that I could not possibly follow.

"Je ne comprend pas," I said.

I laboriously translated, and hands and fingers flew in great excitement. "I do not understand. You sign too fast."

> I rage upon the rooftop in Monaco
> Not deaf, not hearing.
> Mariana studies French
> And passes notes in French
> I study signs and pass my signs

To patient comprehending friends.
Do we attempt to be what we are not?
Or are we searching for ourselves,
For new dimensions of ourselves?
And will our common schizophrenia
Add self-fulfilling struggle
To the search for self?

I light another Caporal
Culture-shock upon a rooftop in Monaco.
My deaf friends join me on the roof.
We sign together in the summer sun
And take each others' pictures
Against the backdrop of the Cote d'Azur.

Mary was my last patient of the day. I ran my fingers through my hair and leaned back in the chair. The late afternoon sun was streaming through the window, reminding me to get curtains to block out the sun. It had been a problem positioning the desk and the patient's chair so no one would have a back to the light. How dependent we are on sight, I sighed.

"Teach me to love myself."

"You and me both, Mary," I said to myself with a wry smile. I glanced down at the lower right hand desk drawer that contained my own "life history": journal clippings, assorted papers, letters, things I had filed away in chronological order for no other reason than I couldn't throw them away. That must have been my father's influence: "Never throw away books and papers," he said, and more by example than words. I recalled with a smile that he even had a "joke file" that he would consult when he needed a touch of humor for a sermon.

....

I looked over on the top of the bookcase at the three-tiered frame holding the pictures of my sons. I was glad I had replaced Mark's stiff crew-cut college graduation picture with informal snapshots from his wedding last spring. No, not his graduation picture—he had long hair for that—but his passport picture, taken when he was sixteen, the summer he was a foreign exchange student. Crew-cut, yes, but bland and so serious. Still serious in the informal shot, sitting at a grand piano in the church before the ceremony, playing out his nervousness as I have heard (seen!) him do so often before. Bless him, I thought, in his first job, teaching math to seventh graders. Denny's picture was more contemplative; perhaps he was thinking of the upcoming bar exam. Jay looked calm and assured, holding a pipe, every inch the Professor of American Lit. How like Jim he is.

Jim. I opened the bottom drawer and pulled out a bulging folder.

two

WHAT SCRIPT?

Although there was little in that folder that dated back further than seven or eight years, I referred to it as my "life history," possibly because previous to that time I had taken life pretty much for granted and was not particularly prone to contemplative or analytic moods. Anything I had written down before that was more likely to have a pragmatic basis, unrelated to my emotional condition. I did write light verse from time to time, usually when I was ironing, since ironing bored me. Before the days of miracle fabrics, keeping my four men in fresh shirts was a necessary but rather unstimulating activity, so I often composed what I called "ironing board poetry" during the chore. Occasionally I wrote small "ditties" for my choir, leaving the ironing board to try them out on the lower half of the piano keyboard, which I could still hear. This "ironing board poetry" was usually directed to some specific event like a housewarming, or the retirement of a significant person in town, or to a fellow sufferer in the school arena after a particularly humiliating defeat of some issue of considerable educational importance. My friend Blaine, the County Superintendent of Schools, was the recipient of one such "opus" that I encased in a giant size capsule that Jim got as an advertising gimmick from some drug company. I had placed the capsule on Blaine's desk after the school district organization election went down to defeat. "To tranquilize you when you deal/With all your fractious districts/Just take this handy king-sized pill—/To hell with all statistics." Blaine sent a message back: "Holly, teach me to iron."

No, the stuff in my folder is much more intense than that. I knew I would need to search back in memory for antecedents to my present dilemma, but I was uncertain how to begin. Though I knew it is possible to analyze oneself, I felt no burning desire to free-associate on paper, and I had a hunch that my own neurotic traits would interfere with valid interpretations. I had read enough psychology to know that the answer could probably be found in my relations with my parents during the first five years of life, and had nothing to do with deafness per se. Moreover, I also knew that what I think has little to do with what my parents intended, but a great deal to do with what I had perceived as their intent. Very young children have not learned to separate fantasy from reality, and when they think they need the fantasies to survive, these impressions can become deeply imbedded into personality and resurface in distorted ways long after the original incident is forgotten.

I recalled a paper I had written in graduate school dealing with Adler's suggestion that a good starting place for self-analysis might be the earliest remembered experience with each parent. Something invariably planted those experiences in the memory, and that something was probably a "survival" feeling. To a small child "survival" often means pleasing Mom and Dad, without whose attention she could not survive.

In another paper, a critique of Berne's Transactional Analysis, I discussed his theory that our destiny is programmed into use in our early years by parents, that we receive a "script destiny," usually by the time we are six years old.

A script? Is carrying out parental directions the purpose of life? There are hierarchies of decisions, I remembered Berne saying. And the highest level is the decision to follow—or not to follow—our script, and until that decision is made, all other decisions will not avail to change our ultimate destiny.

Yet scripts go back to parents' scripts and grandparents' scripts and back way beyond the reach of memory. Symbolically back to Adam and Eve, I suppose, where conscience and guilt were conveniently identified and programmed by Parental Directive.

I felt I had a focus now. So I started the long journey back and found a refrain from A. A. Milne echoing through my mind: "Have you been a good girl? Have you been a good girl? Have you been a good girl, Jane?"

....

My earliest childhood memories were of Goat Island, a Navy Receiving Station then, now the island linking the two sections of the San Francisco-Oakland Bay Bridge. My father was a Navy chaplain, and I could still see the interior of the small chapel on the island; that was sharper than the memory of the interior of our home. I left the sand box (and possible the less-than-eagle-eye of the baby-sitter) one Sunday morning and went to church, parading down the center aisle in my dirty coveralls to take a front seat. Father stopped his sermon to look down at me. "OK, Holly," he said. "You can stay, but sit still or you'll have to leave." Then he continued his sermon. Pondering this memory, I was sure I did sit still; I always felt a tremendous urge to please my father, who seemed like God Almighty, standing up there in the pulpit and saying all those important things. "You certainly favor your father," people would say, "those brown eyes, those heavy eyebrows, that stocky build." I was pleased to look like him, but nobody would ever see me standing in a pulpit. I wouldn't know what to say.

My strongest memories about father always place him in the pulpit. "Listen to me," he seemed to be saying. "Listen to me. I have something important to say." So I listened, and sat still, and couldn't talk back, not with Father up there in the pulpit. It was a long time before I understood his words, but I could remember the feeling. Father's face was extraordinarily expressive. When he drew those heavy eyebrows down, I knew he was displeased. When he pounded the pulpit I would think, "How angry he is," and feel afraid. When he gave the invitation at the end of the sermon, with the choir softly singing "Jesus, I Come to Thee," I would desperately will the congregation to come forward. I knew it would please him so much if they did. I was so mortified when nobody did, as if he had not saved a single soul that day. I remembered his ABC sermon: A— All sin; B—Behold the Lamb of God that taketh away the sins of the world; C— Come unto me all ye who labor and are heavy-laden, and I will give you rest. I wanted to "come unto him" and ask him to explain all those big words. But I never did. "The words don't matter, Holly," he seemed to say. "It's the spirit that counts." And when he'd draw down those heavy eyebrows, I wouldn't need any words. The feeling was punishment enough.

I wondered if the emotional distance in those childhood memories was significant. Father was away often, and Mother, with three stair-step little girls, could not often pick up and follow, although there was never any doubt in my mind that she always wanted to. He would write to her every day when he was at sea, and Mother would receive great bundles of letters mailed at some port of call. She would read them aloud to us and when she came to the "hmm-m-m" and "hmm-m-m" we knew it was love-stuff and only for her. "Some day," she would say, "you will be grown-up and married and you will get love letters too."

I was the middle child; Alice was fifteen months older and Mary was fourteen months younger. Mother had returned to her parents' home in Missouri to await Mary's arrival, and I was farmed out to a childless great-aunt and uncle who lived in a distant town. I can't recall how long I stayed, but I do remember being told that these relatives wanted to adopt me. How, I wondered, had I reacted when I came home after a long period of abandonment and doting attention and found my place usurped by a new baby sister? That memory is a blank.

"She was a placid child," Mother would say of me. "Never gave us a moment's worry." A thumb-sucker, too, she might have added. "Sit still, Holly, or you'll have to leave," Father said. Mother seemed to have said, "Be a good girl, Holly, or Mother will send you away and get a new baby." I found my mind racing ahead on this "rejection" theme, but I felt unable to deal with it now and pushed the feeling away, wondering if it would resurface later.

....

My first remembered experience with my mother? Small Holly, sitting in a bathtub while Mother scrubbed off paint. Mother had whipped me and there were several red welts on my leg and Mother was crying. "Why are you crying, Mommy? Does your leg hurt, too?"

"No Holly. Mommy's leg doesn't hurt because Mommy didn't put paint in the fish pond."

The details flooded back; the sensuous enjoyment of sitting in the fish pond, pouring out the poster paint, watching the colors blend and accumulate along the edges of the lily pads, seeing the goldfish slowly turn over and discovering that they were white underneath. Had there ever been such joy?

I smiled at the memory and imagined the horror Mother must have felt when she discovered the scene. But what was the significance of this experience? Why had it become fixed in my memory? I was pretty sure that Mother hadn't whipped me when I painted the back door screen with mayonnaise, but I did sense that she had not been too happy about it. Did small Holly decide that you get punished when you have fun? Or wonder if only Mother can decide what fun is? But Big Holly heard something quite different: "I cry when you hurt."

Somewhere in those early experiences, I felt, was an answer to my present dilemma, a reason why my current crisis was not resolved. I had a sneaking hunch that it centered more in my father than my mother. Why was it difficult to get close to Father? Why did I see him up on a pedestal, looking down on me?

He had grown up on a farm in Illinois, the youngest of a large family, although he was the only child of his parents' union. Brothers had married sisters and after the death of one brother and one sister, the widow and widower married, and cousins became step-brothers and sisters. Their only child was Father and his parents were well into middle age when he was born. As was the prerogative in those pre–birth control days, his mother was invalided by his birth, although she lived well into her eighties. His father was stern and God-fearing and the family was poor. Young Raymond was required to do many farm chores, and I remembered being moved to childhood tears hearing him relate how he went to Sunday School with milk from the cows spattered on his shoes, and received only the traditional orange for Christmas.

He was a bright lad, and attracted the attention of a lawyer in the nearby small town, who was like a father to him. This benefactor made it possible for him to go to college, and after he graduated, he attended the Northeastern School of Law where he earned the nickname "Deac" because of his regular church attendance. Then he had a call to the ministry, dropped out of law school, and was the pastor of a Baptist church in Missouri when he met my mother.

He was married, she was not. She was from an adjoining small town and in considerable demand as a soprano soloist on the church circuit, so she was invited to sing for a revival service by the young Wilford Raymond Hall, who was serving his first pastorate. His wife was expecting their first child. Complications arose at term, and neither mother nor daughter survived.

Something made me pause. Was there a script of his own here that Father was not able to acknowledge? Had Father unconsciously established the distance himself? Children cause mothers to become invalids, children cause wives to die. "Child, child, don't get too close." But I felt there was more, and forced my memory in this direction, shaken by the sudden insight.

Being a forthright man, he chose Adnee Wright for his second wife. He called on her asking permission to become better acquainted as he intended some day, he said, to ask for her hand in marriage. Mother was startled and explained that she was already engaged to another man, but he did not see this as a particular obstacle, and pressed his suit.

He was successful. Adnee was restless with small town life; her parents had recently embraced the Jehovah's Witness faith and were preparing for the "end of the world." Her world was just beginning and she had no intention of giving it up, so when the young minister joined the Navy during World War I, she married him and they moved to California.

She wanted a big family—and fast—and three daughters were born in a little more than three years of marriage. I had heard the story of my conception and birth and it assumed a special poignancy now. I was conceived during his convalescence following a close brush with death during the post-war flu epidemic. As she approached term Mother had been in the hospital with the same flu. When father received a frantic call to "come quick" he must have felt the tortures of the damned in his race to the hospital. But instead of finding a moribund wife, he found that I had made an early appearance. Another insight: could the circumstance of my conception and birth have been the cause of my hearing impairment? I had wondered, as a child, why they put the half dozen upper keys on the piano keyboard, when they made no sound. I didn't think to ask if anyone else could hear them, and none of my piano music went that high.

What had been relevant about my growing up years? Somehow I needed a clearer picture of my parents and how they related to each other and to me in the context of the family. Somewhere in that matrix might be some answers.

three

Who Says I'm Deaf?

There is nothing in the folder that relates directly to the next phase of my life, but the events are stamped so indelibly in my memory that I need no written reinforcement to recall them. The college years represented the dramatic focus on the onset of deafness.

Music was my major in college, and sometime during my junior year I realized that the high tones were gone. My roommate, Rae, played the violin. I heard the harmonics--but suddenly they were not there. The bow scraped across the strings with a rasping sound, but there was no tone. About the same time I felt that people were not speaking clearly--I had no problem with the volume, but I found myself wishing that they would "take those marbles out of their mouths." I was daydreaming in Dr. Knoles' "World Today" class, and when we got together to study for the final, the others talked about the "Rome-Berlin Axis" and I had been living in my own little world. "What is the Rome-Berlin Axis?" When people whispered, it was as if nothing had been said.

I saw a doctor who did a superficial examination with a tuning fork and could find nothing wrong. The silent six upper keys on the piano had become the whole upper half of the keyboard. Perhaps I had always had some high frequency deafness, but not enough to detect without sophisticated equipment.

....

Father had always been musical in a somewhat untrained way, and music was an integral part of the fabric of family life. Father had earned college expenses playing the piano in a nickelodeon theater and during the later years of his life could still beat out a mean ragtime. He frequently accompanied Mother's solos. Singing for fun was a family recreation, and somehow I had inherited Father's ability to improvise on the piano. I had no formal music training prior to my college experience, but I had a keen desire to learn.

I wondered if I might have "strained" my hearing in Russell Bodley's second year harmony course; that course required intense and selective listening, but I knew that really didn't make sense. That same Russell Bodley had told me, when I tried out for the *a capella* choir, that I had a range of three octaves (I couldn't have been deaf then!), but my most comfortable range was in the low frequencies, so I was assigned to the second alto section.

When I did see a competent specialist, I was not prepared for what he said. I was told that I was severely deaf, that a hearing aid would not help, that it would probably become worse, and I would just have to learn to live with it.

I paused, and tried to re-experience the feeling when I heard that diagnosis. As I recall, the primary feeling was rage and denial. Surely that audiologist must have explained how sound becomes distorted but does not completely disappear when the high tones are gone.

And actually, I suppose, anger and denial were better than depression. I suspect I was afraid to believe it, and did not seek a second opinion for confirmation of the diagnosis. But I did panic, and dropped out of school.

But grim determination soon replaced the panic. Okay, Holly, it's up to you. Nobody else will do it for you. Get back in there and prove you can do anything you want to. Who says I'm deaf?

I transferred to UCLA and completed the music major by the skin of my teeth. The music I wrote for Form and Analysis at College of the Pacific served very well for Composition at UCLA, but the grades were different. I made the *a capella* choir without a tryout, coasting on my reputation at COP. I did not hear the announcement of a quiz, and failed the quiz, so thereafter I always sat in the front row in each classroom.

I did have a moment of triumph.

Guest conductor Albert Coates worked with the UCLA *a capella* choir in a concert version (from manuscript) of his opera "Gainsborough's Dutchess," and during a rehearsal he stopped the choir and pointed at me.

"Did you sing that e-flat?"

"Yes," I said, flustered.

"Well, when I wrote a note that low, I didn't think any woman could really sing it."

Who says I'm deaf!

....

And I met Jim. We both belonged to the same Co-op at the YWCA. Jim was the only male living there, although the Co-op was co-ed for eating purposes. Jim was working his way through college and had a room backstage in the auditorium in return for janitor work in the building. I frequently used the piano in the auditorium for my homework. I could hear the lower half of the keyboard and would write in a lower key and transpose on paper later. Jim would hear me at the piano, slip out from backstage and sit on the piano bench, and talk about life in general, and our love lives in particular. I could manage very well at that time, if I looked directly at the person who was talking. Jim was dating my roommate and I was dating an intern from the County Hospital and Jim was a pre-med. We had a great deal in common and became good friends.

We didn't become serious until sometime later. After graduation, I was casting about for what I could do with a BA in music and abysmal hearing, and recalled that I had scored high on service-oriented occupations in the vocational interest survey. So I applied for a YWCA position in a central California City, sailed through the interview, and was hired.

The job was a nightmare, interspersed with tension dreams and missed cues. I was corresponding with Jim and saw him when I went home for Christmas and Easter vacations. Romantic interest replaced platonic friendship. Suddenly, Jim became my salvation. I was getting love letters too!

Looking back, I find myself wondering about unconscious motivations at that time in my life. Certainly I must have seen Jim as a beautiful way out of my dilemma. After all, sisters Alice and Mary were married and there I was, twenty-two years old and unmarried. Mother was becoming restive: was I going to marry? Nonsense, I thought, I loved Jim. He was so intellectual and articulate. And a doctor's wife "served humanity" too, I thought at the time. I do recall feeling some anxiety about how, in the long run, Jim would deal with my probably progressive deafness he was such a verbal person. But it didn't seem to bother him before we were married, so I pushed my anxiety aside and planned a big wedding. Father proudly marched me down the aisle, and then turned to face us and read the marriage ceremony.

"With a father's blessing, I give you, Holly, to you, Jim."

In my mind's eye, I saw the formal wedding portrait. I am standing gracefully in ivory satin with a train and Jim is looking stiff and somewhat uncomfortable in his PFC uniform. World War II was on, and the Army had put the medical school class in uniform, on inactive status until their education was complete. Jim didn't look very happy in that uniform; turtlenecks suited him better, and of course the beard came much, much later. His hairline had already started to recede; in fact he had teased me about my reference to his "intellectual forehead" and vowed that it was that particular remark that had tipped the scales to matrimony. "That's the kind of a girl that I should marry," he told himself. (The kind of a girl, and not the girl? Should, not want?) Because he was thin, he looked taller than his five feet ten inches, to top me by three inches, which gave him a look of "being in charge of the situation" in the portrait, as did his firm chin. "I know who's going to be the boss in that family," said a friend, looking at the portrait. The thin lips above the chin also had a firm look about them, but the eyes were the dead give-away, so prone to twinkle with dry humor when he was amused, so easily moved to tears by great literature, poetry, fine films, so steely when he was displeased. Jim had maintained his 136-pound weight (we had weighed the same when we were married) and twenty years later, he could still wear his college tux. I sighed, pondering my own fifteen pounds of middle age spread. Would I ever get down to a size twelve again?

As I thought about the early years of marriage I experienced a feeling of warmth and fulfillment. Sure, there were rough spots, but we were young and flexible and could turn them into growth experiences. My hearing loss was pretty stable for almost thirty years, and I learned to make good use of the normal hearing I had in the lower registers. My lip reading skills also helped and I was getting pretty good at reading body language. I continued to deny my deafness, and most of my friends and associates did not realize I had a problem, or if they did, they didn't say so.

Jay was born nine months and twelve days after we were married (people counted on their fingers in those days!) and before we were really ready for parenthood. Jim was only making $40 a month as an intern at the LA County Hospital and Jay's arrival was poorly timed, as Jim was taking State Boards and I felt rather neglected; I had wanted to share the experience of the first born.

Somehow we managed during that lean time. I had work as a bookkeeper for a local school district, took very little maternity leave, and left Jay with Mother when I returned to work. I stopped work when Jim started his residency in internal medicine; you could live on $150 a month in those days. The two years of required Army service was a financial bonanza, and by the time Jim finished medical school, the war was over. Denny was born in Newport News, Virginia, when Jim was stationed at Fort Eustis. This birth was a shared experience, and I felt loved and cherished. It was an added bonus when I discovered what a marvelous father Jim was. We shared the joys and responsibilities of parenthood; I had never been happier.

Jay was a serious little guy, blue-eyed and towheaded, a carbon copy of Jim at that age. He and his Dad developed a startlingly precocious relationship during their long, rambling walks over the Virginia countryside, while Denny and I were occupied with more mundane things at home. Although Jay didn't talk much, he appeared to listen intently, as if he was storing away all those important things his Dad was saying in order to use them at some future time. His first sentence didn't come until he was almost two and it was "'read a book,'" a remarkable harbinger of things to come, I realized, thinking of my Professor of American Lit, off in search of his golden fleece.

Denny had dark hair and dark eyes, a quixotic grin and a long, rangy build. A busy, busy child, who ran instead of walked, and was tender with people and animals. The boys were less than two years apart, and a study in contrast: Jay so fair and Denny so dark; Jay the serious one and Denny the effervescent child.

When Jim returned to his residency, his hours were long and his responsibilities heavy, and his health broke down. He was hospitalized with a pleural effusion that was assumed to be tubercular in origin, and was a patient in the Veteran's Hospital for six months. I put the boys in nursery school and found work in the production analysis department at Douglas Aircraft, a job that lasted until the boys came up with positive TB skin tests and the nursery school would no longer keep them.

I had taken the boys, then two and four, to the pediatrician for further tests and the doctor gently suggested that I remain in the waiting room while he performed gastric analysis. I knew this meant a tube down their throats, and during the interminable wait I was fighting back tears. (Why are you crying, Mommy? Do your legs hurt, too?) Denny finally exploded into the waiting room like a cork from a champagne bottle, a wild look on his face. Jay soon followed, more slowly. and peered up at my face. "Are you happy, Mother?" he asked. I felt the sting of tears again as I recalled that time. Jay was to ask that question again and again over the next few months. No, I wasn't happy really, I was worried and upset, but Jay was so sensitive to this that I would smile through my tears, as I had done in the doctor's office, and say, "I'm feeling a little sad now, Jay. Why don't we all go out and get an ice cream cone, then we'll feel better."

But how much better it became, and how fast! For a convalescent year, Jim took a job as company doctor for a lumber camp in the Sequoia National Forest. What a delightful year that was! It was a beautiful setting, a small town in the middle of the forest, with a lumber mill, a mill pond, homes for the workers and their families, an elementary school, and a doctor's home and office combined that also included a two-bed "hospital" that we often used to house our visitors.

I was the only "nurse" attendant available to Jim. I helped him deliver two babies and "monitored" pelvic examinations (and sometimes played bridge with the same woman that evening). I got a special credential and taught music in the elementary school, which also included a glee club. I even wrote a school song:

> Hail to thee, our Johnsondale.
> Pride of the pines.
> Give courage to our gallant crew
> And victory is thine
> Above Kern River's waters free
> We honor Johnsondale.

From mountaintop we sing to thee:
Hail! Hail! Hail!

....

I also started a Girl Scout troop, and I still have the tablecloth with all of the scouts' names embroidered all over it.

That year changed our lives; we knew we could never be happy in the city again, so Jim abandoned his plans for a medical specialty and opted for general practice. We traveled the length of California with a map in one hand and the medical directory in another, looking for a small town that was close to the mountains for recreation and close to a city for consultation. And needed another doctor. We settled on Placerville, "Old Hangtown" of Gold Rush days. It was back to nature for the Elliotts, Jim, Holly, Jay, Denny, and before long, Mark.

So with borrowed money and a hell of a lot of faith in Jim's ability, we settled down. Here our real life began; this was what it was all about. I had never lived in one house longer than eighteen months in my whole life; I was determined that my children would start first grade and graduate from high school in the same town. I wanted to catch the flavor of this small town; I wanted to become involved and be a real part of it. In my enthusiasm, I said as much to the neighbor over the back fence.

"Mrs. Elliott," the neighbor said, "When three generations of your family have paid taxes in the county, then I will listen to what you have to say."

"Mrs. Sawyer," I said, "When three generations of my family have paid taxes in this county, I won't be here, and you won't either, so I'm going to say it now."

And I did.

four

Was It Enough?

It took time to build a medical practice, and the struggling years were good. I could still use the telephone—in my right ear, if not my left—which was a blessing, because in those days doctors made house calls and were "on call" at night as well as daytime. When Jim was out on a house call, I had to take messages, and he warned me not to give advice over the phone. "You don't have a license to practice medicine. Just take the name and number and I will call back when I return."

One night, when Jim was on a call far out in the countryside, the phone rang, waking me up. It was a frantic mother. "My baby has a high fever and I need the doctor right away."

"Well," I said, "speaking as one mother to another, what I would do is give the baby half an aspirin and sponge her off with cool water." I had heard him say this many times when the phone rang in the middle of the night. "I'll have the doctor call when he returns."

I gave the message to Jim when he returned and he made the callback. I watched his face change, and he said very little.

"What did she say?" I asked.

"She said 'Oh, I just did what the Mrs. told me to do and the baby's much better.'" He shook a finger at my grin. "Practicing medicine without a license."

We bought an old Victorian house and remodeled as we could afford it. Jim's mother made her home with us and became an integral and working member of the family.

We assumed a more casual approach to Mark's rearing in contrast to the more serious style with the two older boys. Perhaps as a result he became the creative one, a child who would have delighted in painting the back screen with mayonnaise or pouring paint in the fishpond. He did find his own variations, once pushing toothpaste through the keyhole to see if it came out on the other side. He turned on the water upstairs to make a lake on the bathroom floor deep enough to float the contents of the overturned wastebasket. He was spanked for that, I remembered, and I also recalled removing soggy foodstuffs from the closet shelves in the kitchen below. But apparently Mark had not received any particular "survival message," as his ebullient childhood sense of fun continued. It was after he put the kittens in the washing machine and was intently watching them through the square window ("kitties go blip, blip, blip") that we finally succumbed to a television set. We were the neighborhood holdouts, determined that the boys' reading habits would be firmly established before we acquired a TV. We also realized that Jay and Denny were going to friends' homes to watch Saturday baseball games, among other programs, so we decided the time had come. Consequently, Mark's reading for pleasure was slower to develop, except for *Sports Illustrated*, which he devoured by the seventh grade. "Reading was a 'must', not a 'want'" he later said, rather regretfully. Jay, five years older, was, on the other hand, engrossed in books by the time he was six. We were constantly urging him to go out and play. I remember suggesting he try out for Little League Baseball, but he was not particularly enthusiastic. On the morning of the tryouts, I pushed him. "I don't feel good," he said.

"Now, Jay," I said, "Go ahead and try out. Even if you don't make the team, you'll feel better because you tried."

So he went, and announced when he returned several hours later, "Well, I made the team, but I still don't feel good." I finally took his temperature: 102

degrees. What kind of mother are you? I asked myself. Perhaps it was a victory of sorts when he became athletic enough to quarterback and captain his high school football team years later, but whether it was his victory, or his dad's, or even mine in recompense for my earlier mistake, I was never quite sure.

Denny was the one who started the family skiing, announcing in his forthright way when he was about ten years old that he was going to learn, and he had a friend who was going to teach him. Denny had apparently made a conscious decision early on that he was not going to compete with his slightly older brother. Jay was the intellectual. Denny would cultivate athletics. Jay learned the piano. Denny would become proficient on the French horn. And, later, he would teach himself the guitar, and write beautiful songs that I could never quite hear.

Jim, Jay, and Mark soon followed Denny to the ski slopes, but it was a long time before I could make up my mind to follow them. I tried to keep myself satisfied with having a hot meal ready on their return. But occasionally I would rebel at the "good old mother" role, and as a result of one such occurrence, they decided that mother would learn to ski. So at age 42, I joined the "togetherness" sport. That was something of a misnomer, as it was, "Mother, you ski here, and we'll be skiing there, and we'll meet you back at the car at four o'clock." But that was OK, I felt, since one or more of them would often schuss downhill, come to a sudden, enviable parallel stop in a cloud of snow, look me over, say, "Mother, you're doing great!" and whiz off again. I never really mastered the sport, because I had too many built-in prohibitions. Not least were the other skiers. They would claim right of way by shouting "on your right!" or "on your left!" as they barreled downhill and I was always "hearing" them when nobody was there.

Jim and I were both civic-minded, he in city government, I in education. He sensed the need for a new sewer system and was elected to the City Council, eventually becoming Mayor. I worked for school district organization and was elected to the County Board of Education. I was active in PTA and ultimately became a life member of the California Congress of Parents and Teachers as well as honorary life member of Delta Kappa Gamma, an honorary educational fraternity for women. (See, Mrs. Sawyer, I remember thinking; it didn't take us three generations, it took only ten years!)

But perhaps my favorite community activity was choir directing at the Federated Church. Although the music I heard was missing many pitches and dreadfully distorted, I could hear the bass and pattern the rest in my mind. I even attended a choir school, given by John Finley Williamson at the San Francisco Theological Seminary. I figured it would be a good way to augment the Federated Church choir's repertoire. I was meticulously careful not to let him know about my hearing loss, but at one point, I found myself on shaky ground.

....

Each member of the class was required to lead the class in a hymn of his or her own choice. I settled on "When I Survey the Wondrous Cross," not realizing, in the excitement of the moment, how my inability to hear sibilants would affect my speech. I announced the title of the hymn.

Dr. Williamson walked up to me. "Open your mouth," he said. "Lift up your tongue." I complied. "You lisp. When you go home, get your doctor to cut that membrane under your tongue. That will help."

"All right," I said, and poured my heart and soul into the task of leading the group in the hymn as I imaged the music in my head. When we finished, the class stood and applauded. He announced:

"You are a good choir director!"

Who says I'm deaf?

....

I continued directing the church choir for twelve years, also developing a community choir that performed an annual Christmas concert.

I was a Cub Scout Den Mother. One incident stands out in my memory. My pack of rowdies had a project to pick up trash along the banks of the creek that bisected the town. We had gunnysacks and pointed sticks, and the boys fell in with enthusiasm. One found an unopened beer can, poked his stick through the top and began squirting the others. I was horrified. "What will I tell your mothers when you get home smelling of beer?" I can still see those boys, rolling back and forth over the ground, holding their sides in laughter.

And I was active in the town branch of the American Association of University Women, serving a term on the state board as chair of the Committee on the Status of Women. Jim and I reached our zenith the year he was awarded the gold stethoscope "Doctor of the Year" by the Sacramento Medical Society, and I received the "Woman of the Year" award from the local Soroptomists.

As I thought about that list of activities, it occurred to me that there are positive aspects to denial. If I had acknowledged the extent of my deafness, I never could have accomplished most of these things. I worked hard at "fitting in."

....

But my deafness was progressing, and Jim and I were taking divergent paths. Hardly anyone, including myself, realized how deaf I really was. I became adept at rationalizing and dissembling. I would break things down into the parts I understood and the parts I could adapt to. There were many activities that did not require good hearing. I was into gourmet cooking and loved it. In later years the Friday night soup pot was always at the ready for out-of-town high school football players who did not have time to go home on the school bus before the game. The dinner hour was always "talk time," and although I could understand little of the talk, I gloried in the give and take between Jim and the boys.

And dreamed "suffering hero" dreams at night. In these vivid fantasies, which I seemed always to wake up from, I acquired the symptoms of Jim's most recent acute patient, and "suffered" so beautifully, bearing my burden of exotic pathology with a calmness and serenity that belied my "mortal pain" and won the admiration of all. My God, I thought, remembering them with a shock; that was psychopathology. It belonged on the analyst's couch, but there was no one to interpret!

Jim finally prevailed on me to have my hearing tested by the otolaryngologist who was his professor in medical school. So we drove the ten hours to Los Angeles, and on the way back, he said, "I had no idea you were so deaf." At the time, I took that as a compliment and felt he was saying that I dealt with it well. I did not hear the subtext of "My God, what do we do now?" That became apparent later.

In 1967, as popular media portrayed young people "turning on and dropping out" in search of "peace and love," Jim felt a tremendous need to be close to those troubled youngsters, and devoted more and more of his time to counseling. About this time he gave a talk to a group of high school students, at a scholarship awards banquet, I think. Before the talk, Jim had told me that he would share with the kids some of the way that he "turned on." Though I had a seat with him at the head table, I could not understand what he was saying: all I could get was the usual frustrating rumble from the PA system. I watched the faces in the audience for clues, and emotions were palpable, but what were they? I asked Jim about it later, but he hadn't written the talk and made some non-committal reply. Then, I remembered that it had been recorded and I asked the high school principal for a transcription. I leafed through my folder.

Borrowing from Camus, Jim had likened the plight of man to that of Sisyphus. "If you remember your Greek mythology," the transcript read, "you will recall that Sisyphus was condemned by the gods to push a stone up a hill. Whenever he got to the brow of that hill, the gods would come and push that stone to the bottom again and Sisyphus had to start over. Part of his sentence was that he not only push the stone up the hill eternally, but that he realize that it was his fate never to reach his goal. In the plight of Sisyphus, Camus saw modern man, but in the reaction of Sisyphus, he saw man's salvation. It is the rolling of the stone that's important. The brow of the hill is nothing. It is the struggle upwards that challenges us."

I recalled how deeply Jim had read in existentialism and how depressed he had been by Camus' untimely death in an automobile accident. I now realized he was trying to define himself, find himself, and doing that independently of me. He had a strong need to communicate and was doing just that with other people. At the same time, I had been reading, but more and more for escape and denial.

"I'm a square," the transcript continued. "I know I'm a square. I'm so square I'm cubed. But that doesn't distress me. Let me tell you how this square gets his kicks. You take me over to Idaho, put three feet of snow on the mountain, put me on the crest of it, give me a blue sky overhead and a clear day, the temperature about 20 degrees, and six inches of new powder, give me a pair of Hart's Superpros and point me down that mountain. Baby, do I turn on!"

And on my bunny hill at Sun Valley, my thought was, "Baby, it's cold outside!"

"Yesterday afternoon I stood at the surgery table with another doctor. We had under our care a man with a bad gall bladder and a bad heart. We took out the gallbladder and he got along very well. For about three and a half hours we had held that man's life in our hands and we kept it and won. And I tell you, friends, that turned me on."

Yes, he had a reverence for life. And if he lost a patient, particularly a child, he would cry. In that wrenching, agonizing aftermath, I could only temper the grief with: "Sure it's tough. But thank God you care."

"Last Monday morning I stood in the delivery room of one of our hospitals and held in my hands six pounds of new-born girl. The baby was taking her first breath and was covered with blood and slime, and boys and girls, this turned me on.

"I have to admit, that this is a dirty, cold, messy, stinking, nasty, miserable, and abominable world. Why should anyone want to stay in it? That is a very fundamental question we cannot escape. Surely no one who is intelligent, sensitive, alert, and in pretty good society can escape the thought of suicide. Sisyphus is Camus' answer to why we don't commit suicide. In spite of the absurdity of the world, we find something worthwhile in remaining in it. I have no need of hallucinations. This world we live in is a real world; it has so much going on out there that I don't want to face it fuzzy-headed. I want to be a part of it. Really a part of it."

Jim lived on the periphery of medical greatness, which he wanted, but felt he could never attain. "The eternal B student," he called himself. Filed next to his Sisyphus talk, I found a poem written at a medical conference he had attended, probably about the same time.

> Standing in the hallway, glass in hand,
> I watch the men and women coming in.
> Laughter, brittle bright,
> Matching the ice in tinkling glasses,
> Accents of Texas, Oklahoma's twang and drawl,
> Midwest flatness, coastal neutrality, Harvard
> Speaking softly in conscious knowledge
> Of something not known to all
> Of us. Young residents, aware of self too much—
> No longer students, not yet part of us outside,
> Their wives slender in bright dresses, animated,
> Talking brightly, shining brightly,
> Hair coifed in careful, careless fashion.
> One wonders where the children are

And who's on call tonight
And how the babysitter's getting on.

Here are the gray-haired men.
Faces smooth with ruddy health,
Assured, knowing, confident,
Quiet in the calm assumption
Of laurels won and well deserved.
These are the doctors of our time.
Men who do not fear their fellows,
Men who know their worth and are not boastful,
Nor conceited, but finding joy and challenge
In their work, move across the face of America,
Talking, teaching, listening to their fellows,
Imparting skills and knowledge
Won in bitter combat, with a largess
That denies their bitter price.
These are the aristocracy of our land.
Who could say, hearing their easy laughter
The casual turn of phrase, the diffident dismissal
Of pain and suffering, what they have paid
For knowledge?

But I, who stand here in the shadows
Can guess the cost; the years of work;
The aching backs, the eyes suffused
From lack of sleep, the agony of failure,
The private hell of patients lost, of mistakes made
With every good intent, the ceaseless trips
Down blind alleyways, the long road back,
The midnight darkness when you say
"But I was wrong," and go back in the room
Everyone around you knowing; trying to pick up
Pieces of a life, trying to make it whole,
Or patch it into something better.

Oh yes, I know, and knowing do not
Begrudge your tailored suits,
Your faces smooth and ruddy
From the sun and drink,
Your easy laughter. For you have paid the price.
None there is among you
Who has not looked at hell and walked
There all alone; none there is among you
Without his private secret, knowing the abyss,
And carrying that dark knowledge deep within.
Emptying my glass I go in among you
Knowing we are brothers.

It was typical of his introspection, and typical of the way he steeled himself to combat his self-doubts. But how much of it was depression?

He was not sharing his feelings much with me, and I found it difficult to reach him. Still, I was not prepared, when sitting on a beach in Oregon, watching the waves advance and retreat, he asked for a separation. I could not believe he was serious, and in my anguish, I wrote a poem to him:

I am a Haven
Penelope reknitting her sweater
Waiting for Ulysses to return
Is it enough?

O strong, dark, brooding man
What are the secret places in your heart?
The ones I cannot reach?
Those lived vicariously in tragic Grecian drama,
The wild dark music of the shades of hell
Absurdity of life; the restless, ceaseless searching
What are you seeking?
Why this strong affinity to hell?

"He went consenting to his hell."

Can Havens gather strength and cry
"Seventy times seven times I'll stand

And raise you from your hell"?
Is it enough, enough?

Then briefly we reversed our roles
And his became the hell of Job
And mine the Grecian sacrifice.
He raged. I had profaned the sacrifice,
Distorted dialogue of soul to soul
Transcendent over sex;
A holy sharing of their tragic hell.

I gave him back his self-respect.
Was it enough? My lonely hell of Job
Obscured his hell, enhanced
And drove it to its fullest power
Of great Olympian grandeur.

And could I choose, would I be hell or haven?
Haven presupposes hell—there is no choice.
I am Penelope, reknitting my sweater
Waiting for Ulysses to return.

Unless he goes, there will be no return.
It is enough. . . it is enough.

Now, six years later, I reconsidered the poem. He had cried, I recalled, when I read it to him on a beach in Oregon. Why had I felt I needed to "rescue" him? Did I think he was not strong enough to rescue himself? And was "rescuing himself" precisely what he was doing? I was putting him down, I thought. I couldn't "give him back his self-respect." Only he could do that.

And later, on that same vacation, we had been talking lightly to disguise our pain. "That's a maidenhair fern," I said, as we walked in a Washington rain forest.

"Are you sure?" Jim asked.

"I think it's a maidenhair fern."

"Are you sure?" he asked, again.

"I am not sure of a god-damned thing in the whole god-damned world," I sighed. He grabbed me and held me close.

But Penelope left more and more of her sweater unraveled, filed for divorce, and went back to school. We tried to reconcile. He spent a summer as a volunteer doctor in a Catholic mission in Guatemala, practicing "gut level" medicine to "find himself." Perhaps he did, but when he returned, I could see no place for me—and fled.

five
A Necessary Turning Point

I realized that we had both been restless the previous five years or so—prey, perhaps, to the "My God I'm Almost Fifty" syndrome, a rather common phenomenon when children start leaving home. Jim had seemed overtly restless, while I had masked my anxiety with a false sense of security. Was deafness a mitigating factor? Certainly it had interrupted communication, and if I had been denying the deafness I had been less than true to myself.

Yet, as I looked back over those twenty-four years of marriage I wondered if what I had experienced was really a denial of deafness. In many ways it was easier to be deaf in that environment, protected, as I had been, by loving acceptance of family and friends. I shared an identity. I was "wife," and "the boys' mother," and within that protection I could find a certain identity of my own, with latitude to experiment inside the framework of my disability. I had told myself that deafness was not going to interfere with anything I really wanted to do, but I doubted that I had ever really put it to the test. I suspect that I had rather liked being dependent; it kept me from facing myself. There were so many ways I could compensate creatively. If someone had asked me, I would have said that I gained pleasure from watching other people experience pleasure, and, perhaps, to a certain extent, that was true. Who wants to repeat the punch line of a joke? I laughed with others as if I understood. I was not denying that deafness is stressful to hearing and deaf alike. Hearing people naturally enjoy the spontaneous give and take of conversation, and repetition often kills the spontaneity. Deaf people must impose their condition on others, and I was not willing to do that.

But what about "suffering hero" dreams and the wrenching panic I felt at being thrust upon my own. Be a good girl, Holly, or mother will send you away and get a new baby. Be a good wife, Holly, or Jim will send you away and get a new wife. The rejection theme, I thought, it surfaces again. Was it script fulfillment? Did I unconsciously set myself up for it? Did I find some measure of fulfillment in the role of "victim?"

But Jim was the Ulysses of Kazantzakis, not Homer, and fulfillment was in the search, not the goal. For me, Penelope was only a temporary role. Bruce, my pastor, kept urging me to investigate ways of working with deaf people. But, I kept saying, how could I when my only qualification was deafness itself? And my college major was music? Could I leave the protection of the hearing world and identify as a deaf person? Was that the ultimate test of acceptance?

The question was moot, really. I was a deaf person, I told myself. I was on my own. Economic and emotional expediency dictated the need for a new identity. Would it be a more real identity? Where I could truly be myself? Where my frontiers would be tested in terms of my own abilities and motivations (and limitations) and no one else's? Where I could move at will among deaf and hearing on my terms and at the comfort level I dictated myself?

If my childhood had prepared me for anything, it prepared me for innovation and change, for exploration. So okay, change. In what direction, and where do I start?

I made inquiries about how I could be evaluated for something, and learned that there was a rehabilitation counselor for the deaf in Sacramento. After about half an hour of listening sympathetically to my story, she suddenly said: "Why don't you do what I'm doing?"

"What's that?"

"You go back to school and get a master's degree in rehabilitation counseling."

"How can I do that if I can't hear what goes on in the classroom?"

"That's no problem," she replied. "You ask someone to make carbon copies of their notes."

"Do you mean I can go back to college?"

"Of course you can."

I grabbed this suggestion as if it were a life preserver tossed out on a turbulent sea, and registered at State College in time for the spring semester. I had received my interlocutory decree the previous month and college was a big step toward independence.

....

I smiled a little as I came across another poem I had written about this time. I hadn't kept a copy and it turned up in Jim's effects. I had decided that since conversation didn't work well with Jim, this mode seemed more effective. In place of a title I had penciled across the top, "I've come a long way since the Penelope days."

> New horizons turn the desert of my soul
> Into a fertile field.
> Compassion grows there now.
> The flower of love, un-nurtured, dies.
> Its seeds lie dormant in the ground.
> Gone the slim, bent stalks
> That grasped for strength
> Upon the thin topsoil of illusion;
>
> Reality, with winter's grip, intrudes its icy blast
> And so the flower dies.
>
> Tested are the strengths
> As they were tested oft before;
> And then the final test: "I am myself with no one else."
> The strength all but consumed
> Within the fires of doubt and pain,
> Shook off the ashes
> And arose again.

Perception is the wheel
That spins the thread of my compassion
And knits the raveled fabric of my soul.
The woman is there, her passion stilled
For passion is not all.
To be, to think, to feel, to share
To feel the inner peace,
To find serenity at last.

Passion is a woman, reaching in.
Compassion also is a woman,
Reaching out.

I had attached Jim's response to it when I had found the poem in his effects. "Your note and the poem came yesterday," he wrote. "So far from Penelope is right. I always knew you had deep understanding. I've never known you to express it so beautifully, nor with such grace and power. I'm very confident you will do surprisingly well—surprisingly, only to yourself. I hope this peace of mind you speak of comes soon; I'm sure you will find it; sooner, I hope, than later. There are so much of you yet to emerge and to find yourself, and such a valuable person yet to come. I think of the dragonfly upon a stalk of grass, just emerging from its chrysalis, wings wet, bedraggled, useless. But a few hours in the sun and the wings dry, harden into functional shapes, become iridescent; and shimmering in new beauty, carry their wearer off into a new world of light and air and blue sky and water. Your wonderful facility for making friends will stand you in good stead. I think of so much that you have taught me about people. I need that knowledge and keep it as part of my working tools. Thank you so much."

I felt a warm glow as I read that message again. And I saw the poem now as a manifestation of Erikson's necessary turning point: "It may be a good thing that the word 'crisis' no longer connotes impending catastrophe. It is now being accepted as designating a necessary turning point, a critical moment, when development must move one way or another, marshaling resources of growth, recovery, and further differentiation."

—Erik Erikson, *Identity, Youth, and Crisis*

six

I Want To Go Home and Bake a Good Cheesecake

The next item was my first return-to-college paper and reminded me of how scary it had been to go back to school again; that first semester was a terrifying transition period. I was identifying as a "deaf person" in a college that had little experience with deaf students, and I was left pretty much on my own as far as adjustment was concerned. It was a long drive to the campus and I was continuing to maintain a home for Mark, who was a senior in high school. Commitment to my community activities continued: choir directing, County Board of Education, and state committee work. It was as if I was being stretched between two worlds: unwilling to give up one, yet feeling not quite acceptable in another.

On the first day of classes I found myself in a course called "Appraisal in Vocational Rehabilitation Counseling," taught by the psychologist at the local rehabilitation agency. The course was designed to acquaint the student with the psychological tests used for evaluation purposes with rehabilitation clients. We were to discuss the tests, take them ourselves, and, as a final examination, write a paper evaluating our own test results. I had felt that it was a propitious time to take such a course, as I was rather preoccupied with self-evaluation anyway. The first day we were given the Employment Aptitude Survey to evaluate our intellectual potential.

Well. I remember my fear like a vibrating weight in my stomach. Suddenly I had come to a place where I could no longer pretend to hear what goes on. I hadn't computed anything but checkbooks for years and I had been reading for escape for so long that I wondered how much of what I read I could retain. I was determined to do it, but was not all that sure I could. This was no time, I thought, to take an IQ test, or a personality test either, for that matter. My mind was still confusing "who am I?" with "who do I want to be?" and "who do I think I should be?" My confidence was at a low ebb indeed.

My computational score had been abysmal, but the verbal score raised the average to a level the instructor felt would see me through the mental rigors of rehabilitation counseling, so the first hurdle was passed. My "profile" gradually emerged. The vocational preference test revealed that I was probably starting in the right field; my personal-social levels were high and the Kuder Occupational Interest Survey indicated that my interests were consistent with those in the service-oriented fields. The Graduate Record Examination was a requirement that semester, too, but I had time to prepare for that and received considerable coaching in computation from my math whiz of a son. Mark pulled some procedures from my unconscious where they had lain dormant for many years, like what *pi* is and how you figure the area of a circle. Later in the semester I took the Ohio State University Psychological Test and the Concept Masters and was able to pull my IQ score up to a level that was consistent with my undergraduate years. In fact, my score on the Ravens Progressive Matrices had astounded me.

As I started to read the final paper from my folder, I remembered the satisfaction of the whimsical creative kick I was on when I wrote it; it took the form of a dialogue between counselor H. Elliott (Alter Ego) and client Holly E. (Ego). The instructor's comments on my paper were more than kind; she encouraged me to continue writing. "This is the most interesting paper I have read in a long, long chain of journaling this and that," she had written on the face of the paper. "You appear not only to have learned about 'testing' but also about many other things as well. You should keep this paper and reread it at appropriate intervals. You might think of publishing in a journal some day."

How I needed that, I thought, leaning back in my chair. The paper still moved me, was still powerful as it groped to articulate my struggles, the self-doubts that lay behind it. "Listen to me!" I felt myself pleading throughout the paper. "I have something important to say."

....

Counselor was pretty hard on Client.

"Ugh," said Client when they came to the personality tests.

"What's wrong?" asked Counselor. "Were they inconsistent with the other tests?"

"Not they, it, the MMPI. What a horrible test."

"Well," said Counselor, "we don't recommend its indiscriminate use with clients. Only trained psychologists should interpret the results. But it isn't a horrible test at all. It's a very good test. Let's explore your problems. Number one?"

"Number one," said client grimly, "I was in a poor mood to take that test. I had just returned from a women's conference and had been told by the brass to quit rocking the boat. In short, my pet project was shot down. I came home feeling very anti-feminist and anti-establishment."

Counselor was a little impatient. ""If you can calm down, let's see what your profile looks like. Your suppress0r variable was certainly high. You were obviously trying to hide something. But your HS score is low. How do you explain that?"

"Oh, I've never been a hypochondriac. No fun to be sick. No feedback. It's like the cobbler's children, I guess. Even when I was pregnant I didn't have the dewy-eyed expectant father. 'Millions of women have babies,' he told me. 'You'll breeze right through.'"

"Did you?"

"Sure. I'm healthy as a horse except for my abysmal hearing. He did express some anxiety about whether the baby would be normal. He was on the pediatrics ward at the county hospital at the time, and was pretty overwhelmed by some of the congenital anomalies of the newborns he was seeing. 'However,' he said, 'be prepared for eczema. It runs in the family.' We got it. Denny's legs kept getting infected. His first sentence was 'please don't take my banjie off,' poor baby."

"Look, we're talking about you, not your kids," said Counselor. "Let's stick to the subject. Now, D and HY are within normal limits, so we are not concerned with depression or hysteria. Surprised, aren't you? And you're not schitzy, in spite of what you said about 'illusions.' Pd is high, but you may have been reflecting your rebelliousness to authority there. Hey—femininity zooms! What have we here?"

"I wish I knew. As a matter of fact, what I was feeling when I took that test was dissatisfied, driven, and determined. Was I trying to hide it? Was I trying to be more feminine than I am? Something was obviously going on there. That score looks as if I was trying to prove that I am God's gift to husbands. Hah!"

"We'll call it reaction formation, Holly. 'Nobody's going to tell me that I am not a good wife.' Look at your high suppress0r variable."

"Yes, but…"

"He is not telling you that you were not a good wife. He was really telling you that he needs something different, and that's not the same thing."

"Yes, but . . . ."

"And no 'yes, buts.' Just think about it for a while. You probably wanted something different, too, but it's just taking you longer to admit it. Now, Ps is getting on the high side; in fact, it's your highest score."

Client looked worried. "I know, and it bothers me. Does it mean I'm paranoid?"

"Let me tell you something, Holly," said Counselor, looking like a dutch uncle. "Do you remember when you came into the rehab office last fall and were in such anxiety that you couldn't keep the edge of hysteria out of your voice? Do you realize what an MMPI would have said then? And what does it say now? It says that you are no longer hysterical or depressed. It says you have been working on it, that you have found purpose in life again. Don't you remember what Rabbi Heschel said, Holly? That human living is being-challenged-in-the-world, not simply being-in-the-world? That the root of creativity is discontent with mere being? Well, up paranoia! Just remember, you can't win 'em all."

"Yes," said Client gloomily, "but I lost the big one. Besides, I'm going to have to learn to curb that paranoia. What if I decided the State Department of Rehabilitation needed reforming. I'd probably lose my job!"

"Don't worry," said Counselor. "You'll probably be so busy with your clients that you won't have time for the Department. The only thing that worries me is, will you need the clients more than they need you? What you need is to get off that nuturance kick. But, to go on. Pt is right on the norm, so you don't appear to be neurotic, at least no more than average. Ma is rather elevated, but so are the Mas of other creative, active people. You probably need your hypermania now, but it will diminish when you stop trying to 'prove' yourself. It could also be a response to your change in lifestyle; but it also may show that you find it difficult to tolerate conflict or tension states. Right?"

"I guess so," mumbled Client.

"OK, let's look at the overall profile. Your mean score is certainly within the limits of normal. None of your scores go above 70, the critical range. Your Mf score is on the low side, but that probably is a reaction formation caused by your divorce. Now we will look at those three points on the graph where you peak. Those are not high enough to indicate psychopathology, but they might suggest your problem areas: Ma, Pd and Pa. We have already discussed Ma. High Pd and Pa usually indicate hostility, and in the absence of antisocial history (and I wouldn't call you antisocial) this hostility may be considered to be interjected, or turned against the self. Holly, did it ever occur to you that you might be angry?"

"Who, me...?"

"Who me, indeed. That's why your suppressor variable is so high. You seldom show anger and certainly you withhold criticism of others. So you're angry. So what? Isn't that better than being anxious or depressed? Might it not be a realistic response to a difficult life situation?"

"Yes, but . . ."

"I haven't convinced you, have I? Well, let's move on to the Incomplete Sentence Blank."

"You can't have that one."

"What do you mean I can't have it? Didn't you take it?"

"No."

"Why not? I gave you the blank."

"Well, if you must know, I gave it to my seventeen-year-old son. He has been very interested in these tests and he pored over a number of them. I didn't give him any because I had already filled out the answer sheets. However, with the sentence completion I said: 'Here, take this, but write lightly and erase, as I have to take it too. And be sure you answer with the first thing that comes into your mind. Then look it over, you may find something interesting. But then erase so I can take it.'"

"I was getting dinner when he took it," Client continued thoughtfully. "I almost told him he was cheating, he shouldn't take so long. But something held me back, and I delayed dinner. We had dinner and then he went upstairs to do his homework. The test was on my desk and he did not write lightly, nor did he erase. And it was the most beautiful communication I have ever had from my very bright, but rather silent son. He wrote: The best dessert is a good cheese-cake. He wrote: I can't figure out people or unmask their feelings. He wrote: Mothers are very understanding. He wrote: When I was a child I knew nothing of sorrow or hurt. He wrote: Marriage scares me. He wrote: The only trouble is that I don't understand yet. He wrote: What troubles me is that black skin makes any difference. He wrote: I wish war wasn't. He wrote: My greatest worry is that I will always care. And (dear God!): Most women need to be loved.

"No, you can't have that one because that communication was for me. I am not going to erase it."

"Did you talk about it later?"

"No, we didn't need to. Somehow we understood each other without saying a word. But I have to go home now."

"What's the hurry? Your time is not up yet."

"I want to go home," said Client. "I want to go home and bake a good cheesecake."

seven

"When I Am Dead Sing No Sad Songs For Me"

A letter from Denny was the next paper in the folder and it brought back the strange, otherworldly quality of that summer after my first semester at State. Jim had asked for a reconciliation before he left for Guatemala, in a compulsive effort to burn bridges and start over. Jay was at Indiana University where he was working towards his Ph.D. in American Literature. Mark was getting ready for college in Colorado. Both Jay and Denny had been reclassified 1-A by the draft board since student deferments had been abolished due to the Vietnam War. Jim and I had desperately wanted to be a family again, to recapture the remnants of what we had. Jim had insisted that I contact the architect and start plans for a new house on a bluff overlooking the mountains. I sold our beloved Victorian house that summer and Mark and I moved into Jim's apartment awaiting his return. Jim was writing beautiful letters from Guatemala, about the countryside, about the impoverished Indians he was treating. "If you were here," he wrote, "I could live here forever, and die here."

Because of the draft Denny was a Vista Volunteer in Chicago and evoked the chaos there for us.

55

"The march itself was very orderly," he wrote. "We were three abreast in a line that stretched over four blocks. Our objective was to get as close as possible to the Democratic National Convention to show our disgust for the proceedings that had taken place there. Dick Gregory had invited us to his house on the south side near the Convention. For all of those bastards who are concerned with law and order, we were within the law. There were three thousand of us walking calmly down the sidewalk to Gregory's house. At Fifteenth Street, over twenty-five blocks from the Convention, we met about two hundred guardsmen and two hundred more policemen. They announced that nobody could go any farther south because of the uneasy racial situation. What they really meant was that if we had gone any farther south, the Blackstones and all the other soul brothers would have joined us. That was an alliance the cops were anxious to prevent. After about twenty-five people were hauled off in police vans, things were getting a little tight. So out comes the tear gas. They gave us no warning. Just all of a sudden poof, it's there. Cries went out for medics. As I was walking up State Street, back to the Hilton, my eyes were burning like hell and my nose ran like a water faucet. Almost two thousand of us were marching up the middle of the street, tying up traffic and chanting: 'Fuck Mayor Daley!' and 'Kill the pigs!' I was right there with them. I was chanting 'Fuck Mayor Daley' with the same conviction that I had sung 'American the Beautiful' in Grant Park the night before. Tomorrow's sun will dull my memory, while the newspapers will act as if nothing had happened. Yet I know, when I lie down to sleep tonight, tomorrow night and the next night, I will see lines of blue shirts, silver helmets, bayonets and jeeps, Mayor Daley and Hubert Humphrey. I hope my rage never dies."

I thought of the Bantu Sage when I reread Denny's letter. "I have begotten a son. I will live on in him. Go, my son, and mix with the crowd."

I read the carbon copy of my reply in which I tried to bolster him with the cautious optimism I was feeling. "Man is a 'bad weather' animal, Denny, which is another way of saying 'the fittest survive.' What is going on now must go on, but the Daleys, the Nixons, the Johnsons and the Humphreys are the last of their breed. They are the old men. Sure, we'll have to endure it for another four years, but that will increase the rage, unite the social forces, and soon kids like you will be taking over. And you won't be kids. You're not kids now. I hope I live long enough to see it, for the day will come. And I will know that my sons, and their sons, and their sons will in some measure be responsible for that new day."

Yes, I thought, Denny's letter had contributed to the quality of unreality during that summer of '68. After Jim's return from Guatemala, he, Jay, who was back from the Midwest, Mark and I had crowded into Jim's small apartment.

Jim's eyes were fever-bright as he talked, and talked and talked, far into the night, of his Guatemala experience.

After Jay returned to Indiana, after Mark was put on a plane for college in Colorado, the house of cards collapsed. The relationship was without substance or depth. We had both started on new paths, and I realized that you really couldn't go home again. I moved to a motel to ponder my next move and when I registered for the fall semester it suddenly hit me that I didn't have an address.

....

Looking back I ask myself: was deafness the mitigating factor? And I must respond "yes." Jim needed the support of easy communication; I needed to identify myself as a deaf person. I was forty-eight, and still had the potential to develop a career. We both needed change. Our parenting years were over and we both needed to go separate ways. It took time for me to realize this; the break-up of a marriage is painful and I had contributed my share of passive-aggressive behavior. My regret is that we did not part on a supportive, friendly basis.

The next paper in my folder shocked me. I knew it was there but had not wanted to face the fact that it was so close. Jim's poem, the one he wrote sometime after his return and announced that he wanted read at his memorial service. Did he have a premonition then?

> When I am dead
> Sing no sad songs for me
> Nor read above my grave
> A litany of sonorous sound

That muffles in mellifluous tones
The simple fact that I am dead.

Wail not for my supposed soul
Fixed in some sea of fiery trial
Awaiting Lazarus' touch.
The trial of life is fiery sea enough
And man need seek no future hell
Greater than that he makes here
In his own good time.

Heaven and earth,
The evolutionary turmoils of the past
Future hopes and present times alike
Are bound in this somatic form
Which holds the wondrous stuff of germinal epithelium
Continuous since the times of
Ancient mystery when vague forms
Moved within the deep
And ancient atmospheres and seas
Spawned forth complex nucleic acids
And Ancient Gods looked down
And saw that they were good.

Consider then the mystery: particles of DNA
Mine by inheritance, fragmented,
Added to by others and sent to spin
Their webs of cellular destiny
Retelling the old, predicting the new
That will be old; forcing their imprint
On the pattern of the future;
Working their silent, subtle ways
in my three sons.

This then is my estate:

No broad expanse of lawn or hill
No treasures locked within deep vaults,
Nor towers, nor halls, nor yet bronze plaques
Commemorating useless dates,
But living sons. And this my legacy.
And this my epitaph:
He loved life, and loving, lived.

So Jim died of hepatitis on December 7, 1968, one month before the divorce was final. He had carried a virulent form of the disease home with him from Guatemala and it had smoldered and smoldered, then erupted. I had not known he was sick until a few days before he died. I saw him in the hospital, tormented, thrashing, but he did not know me.

The boys were summoned, Jay from graduate school in Indiana, Denny from Hull House in Chicago, and Mark from Colorado College. Jim's mother and sister came up from the southern part of the state. They all stayed with me in my rented home and went to the hospital in shifts. On that last night, when the rest of the family was standing the deathwatch, I was at home alone, on the floor in front of the fireplace, writing a poem. The death of a marriage is hard; the death of a loved one is harder still.

Why was Never Never Land denied?
He was a questor
Ulysses searching for illusive goals.
Perhaps for a brief time
He found what he was searching for
And in the finding incubated
Seeds of his destruction.

He fought. In life and death he fought.
His sons in their magnificence
Fought with him 'til the last small flame
Was gone.
And how he fought
That vast array of medical technology

That kept his life a flickering flame.

Death was often his companion.
His prayer: "God give me strength
To die with dignity."
He went consenting,
"When I am dead
Sing no sad songs for me."
And were his final thoughts of Never Never Land
A goal achieved?

And I, his widow,
I, who bore his sons,
Sustained and loved him through the years
Was in the end denied his death.
The death that wipes out Never Never Land
And brings him back.
Briefly he touched his horizon.
Perhaps it was enough.

The day after he died, my Christmas Choir was scheduled to give its annual
concert. Although I was emotionally spent, I felt compelled to go through with
it. Jay and Denny were in the audience, as were Jim's mother and his sister. Mark
had to go back to college for finals. I could still feel the spiritual ecstasy of that
final anthem, the Prayer of St. Francis:

O divine Master
Grant that I may not so much seek to be consoled
As to console.
To be understood as to understand
To be loved as to love.

It was the last concert I was to conduct.
Jim's ashes were interred in a little Guatemalan cemetery on a broad hill
with a vista, a place he had called "the most beautiful spot in the world." The

Indians celebrated a Mass for the repose of his soul, although he was not Catholic.

And I went back to my interrupted paper for Theories of Counseling. "Write a paper on your own philosophy of life" the instructor said. "You have to know yourself before you can help other people." I read what I had written and tore it up. I had experienced life and death so deeply since I had put that assignment aside two weeks before. Old words would no longer suffice.

eight

Suicide or Crucifixion?

It was some time before I went back to my folder again. The memories evoked by those documents had left me deeply shaken, and I needed some distance to gain perspective. When I finally pulled out the paper that I had turned in for the "Theories of Counseling" class, I realized how strongly the Parental Directives had come through. Should I be a psychotherapist? I had written as if I hadn't known if I really wanted to be a therapist, but the Parental ego state was telling me that I should. I sighed and settled down to read the paper.

....

Should I be a psychotherapist?

It's the eternal question: who am I and where am I going? Rabbi Heschel said that "we cannot reflect about the humanity of man and retain a relationship of complete detachment, since all understanding of man is derived from self-understanding, and one can never remain aloof from one's self." Before becoming a psychotherapist it is necessary to face yourself, your anxieties, inhibitions and behavior traits that make life difficult, and sometimes impossible. A psychotherapist must learn how to find the way out of the labyrinth of his/her own emotions before he/she can help other people.

For a deaf person, the communication process itself can be a labyrinth of blind alleys, wild guesses, and dead stops. Yet, communication is more than sound. Carl Rogers asked himself: "Can I hear the sounds and sense the shape of this person's inner world? Can I resonate to what he is saying so deeply that I can sense the meaning he is afraid of, but would like to communicate?" In discussing what he calls the "Third Ear," Theodore Reik tells us that the therapist must learn how one mind speaks to another beyond words and in silence. You don't have to shout to make yourself understood. Listen to the expression, the meaning behind the words. So often words are a mere mask of feeling. Don't let your anxieties interfere with listening; don't get hung up on words. And yes, words are fundamental to the communication process whether they are spoken, heard, lip-read, signed, or written. Communication is more than words, but the words are there to be interpreted.

....

Is my experience with deafness something that would be worthwhile to share with other people? Deafness is so misunderstood, so stressful to deaf and hearing alike. My experience has been compounded of trial and error, which has included denial, despair, stoicism, and distortions in personal relationships, along with occasional successful resolutions.

But what is success? By society's standards, success is the attainment of wealth, favor, or eminence, but I do not aspire to any of these. Success can only be measured in terms of the individual's own frame of reference. Success for a deaf child may be a word spoken or a meaning understood. The most wealthy, favored, and eminent person is successful only in the measure by which he/she has attained his/her own goals, and achievement is fluid, dynamic, and never-ending. To stop when goals are attained is to die.

Paradoxically, failure is a part of success. "In this world," said Oscar Wilde, "there are only two tragedies. One is not getting what one wants, and the other is getting it. The last is the real tragedy." Eric Hoffer tells us of the uniquely human fact that discontent is at the root of the creative process; that the most gifted members of the human species are at their creative best when they can't have their way and must compensate for what they miss by realizing their capacities and talents.

Success is asking the question: what am I here for? and acting on the answer. The hazard of success (I read somewhere) is that in winning the small prizes, we gamble our lives away. The small prizes are society's acceptance; the large prize is self-acceptance. Success can only be deeply personal to have real meaning. It involves overcoming barriers, including failure, to reach the goal.

So I ask myself: Okay, Holly, can you combine experience, awareness, and communication and come up with a congruent whole? I am reminded of a lesson I learned years ago in a class in music composition: you have to learn the rules before you can make the value decision on how to break them creatively.

Experience? A full life—and baptism by fire. Deafness at age nineteen and reconstruction. Building a home, reinforcing my basic philosophy, and seeing it reflected mirror-like in the personalities of my three sons. The active years in our small town: president of this and that, school board, bond drives, choir directing, legislative advocate, state committees, ski weeks at Sun Valley, education-woman-of-the-year, Soroptimist-woman-of-the year, parties, big, big frog in little, little pond. Who says I'm deaf?

The Penelope years: reknitting my sweater, waiting for Ulysses to return. And the ultimate failure: divorce. And the ultimate loss: death.

"Fortitude," my friend Susan wrote, "has a long background of success, when, after the initial and sometimes continuing rage, it sees you through to better times. It makes you happy, once you have overcome, that you had it. It gives you strength in your beliefs, and belief in yourself. It gives you pride in your strength."

Awareness? Two human qualities seem necessary: perception and compassion. My oldest son, Jay, wrote "No longer do I hope to return to those pleasant days of ignorance, nor hope to pull down the mist of pre-perception. An increase in perception brings pain. But after the psychological warp: triumph. I can use the perception instead of having it oppress me. I can choose to reveal myself now, where before oppression goaded me. With freedom, perspective has returned. And with perspective, a sense of well-being."

And I wrote: "Perception is the wheel that spins the thread of my compassion, and knits the raveled fabric of my soul."

Communication? Ay, there's the rub! Listen, Holly, a feeling process, and a thinking process. Listen, as Rogers does, for the deep human cry that lies buried and unknown far beneath the surface; the visceral reactions and feelings as well as the thoughts and words. Listen without judging, diagnosing, appraising, evaluating. Listen to what he is really saying, not what you want him to say. Rogers, where were you ten years ago?

The only way to find out is to try. Like Sisyphus, I'll keep pushing that stone up the mountain as I become involved with humankind on a wider scale.

Not long ago, two very wise young men asked me how I planned to die. I was shocked, as I was much too involved with living to contemplate dying. "There are only two ways to die," they said. "By suicide or crucifixion." I still did not understand. "When you stand in front of that six foot hole and look back--what's it going to be? Suicide or crucifixion?" Then I understood. They were not talking about death—they were talking about life. "He who loseth his life will find it."

Defining man, my youngest son, Mark, wrote: "If he states a doctrine, he must live by it if he thinks it is right. If he is wrong, he must face the consequences due. When he makes a mistake, he must be responsible for it. And when he meets death, he must go consenting."

I like to think I have that kind of courage. When the next twenty-five years have passed, I'm not going to stand in front of that hole and look back. "For looking back," wrote my middle son, Dennis, "is the sin punishable by a slow death of the imagination, like the river that is forced by dams to cease its work of exploration and rest immobile." I've already chosen my path, and it won't be suicide.

It takes faith, faith in the process of life. I'd like to think I have the courage, twenty-five years from now, to ride the lift up the highest mountain I can find, strap on my skis, and head down hill, full bore with wax on.

nine

"Don't Be Close"

I had a vague feeling of discomfort about the next paper in my file, and almost decided to toss it, wondering why I had saved it in the first place. I remember my eagerness (or was it fear?) when I went to pick up the transcription of the presentation; I also remember some feeling of embarrassment when I read the transcription, as if it had not faithfully reproduced my emotional reactions. I wondered if now, six years later, I would see something in it that escaped me then.

The tape was from a seminar in Group Processes, and I never really felt comfortable in that class. The instructor organized the seminar into a therapy group, and the purpose was to share our own particular hang-ups with the other members of the class. Each student was asked to write a contract involving his own hang-up and how it might be resolved, then share it with the group. I had no trouble identifying mine; being in the group itself was trouble enough, since most of the time I didn't have the faintest idea what they were talking about, so I made myself as inconspicuous as possible. It was a required course, but pretty much a waste of time as I saw it.

I remembered being pleased with my written contract; I felt it had expressed quite well the way I was feeling at the time. Re-reading it was a shock. I seemed to have swung from too few words of my own to too many.

"One of the biggest problems I have to face is a terrible sense of alienation in a group. It's not that I can't empathize—I think I can—but, as Rogers says, real communication implies congruence, and in my case, as with all deaf people, I can't communicate unless the other person really wants me to hear what he or she has to say. Therefore, a group is a threat to me. Sometimes I have to make myself come to this class, and one time I decided I was too busy to come, and afterward wondered if that was the real reason.

"Deafness is very isolating. This is implicit not only in the deafness per se, but also what is known as 'shock-withdrawal-paralysis.' This last, I believe, is not really conscious on the part of hearing people, but happens because it is so much easier not to talk with a deaf person. After all, there are so many other people who can react instantaneously to what you have to say. No problem about immediate feedback. We are perfectly willing to do that for deaf people—but with deaf people?

"Now I am perfectly aware of the fact that this is my problem, not yours. I don't want people to communicate with me from a sense of responsibility because I am deaf, or because I am a member of this group. I do want people to communicate with me because I am a human being and because I might have something to say. Therefore, I am asking you to ponder on this for a few days before the next class session. I want to hear your ideas, and I would like your reactions to some of the ways I think this problem can be alleviated. I want to bring a tape recorder to the next class session and record our honest reactions to this problem that is so universal among deaf people.

"In the first place, the deaf person is rather reluctant to make a 'thing' of his/her deafness when associating with hearing people. There is a temptation, with this invisible handicap, to try to pass as hearing. This, believe me, is disastrous, and involves all those psychic problems that are associated with denial of self. Therefore, the deaf person must make the major adjustment. A certain amount of just plain acceptance is necessary. You're not going to hear much of what's being said in a group. That's just the way it is. So why be defensive?

"But withdrawal is not the answer. If not withdrawal, what? I believe that the deaf person must take the initiative in the communication process. There are risks involved; the risk of inappropriate responses, the risk of dominating the conversation, of compulsive talking because if you stop you are afraid the other guy will start and you won't know what he is saying. But that is monologue, not communication. If he/she doesn't establish it him/herself, it is very important for the deaf person to find the context. Once that is established (and it sometimes takes a while—a cue here, a cue there) he/she can make his/her contribution to the communication process. Immediate feedback would be, to the deaf person, setting the stage for one-on-one communication, which is about all he/she can manage, anyway.

"It is important for the deaf person to place him/herself in the other person's frame of reference. If she forgets herself and concentrates on the other person, she is far less likely to worry about words, words, words. If she tries too hard to get the words, all those units of energy needed to translate words into meaning are used up by stress. She can empathize with the other person by concentrating on how he says it as well as what he is saying. The words will come more easily if the self is minimized, and consequently, stress is reduced.

"I cannot overemphasize the value of a sense of humor. If I feel stress, so will the person with whom I am trying to communicate. Keep it light, Holly. Laugh at yourself.

"Much has been written about the widespread and pernicious problems of 'paternalism' that enmesh deaf people. Deafness is sometimes equated with stupidity. I believe it is incumbent on the individual deaf person to make very real efforts to improve this image. After all, it's only the deaf person that you don't know who's stupid. So let's get acquainted!

"A deaf person can only hear what he can see. He does not want you to shout at him, or get up close and spit all over him. All he wants is for you to face him when you talk and articulate as well as you can. In a group, of course, he only expects this occasionally. And beyond that, forget that he is deaf, if you can. He will let you know, gently, one hopes, if he does not understand what you are saying. If he has fully accepted that fact of his deafness, all he asks is that you accept it, too. Once the psychic barriers are down, you may be surprised at how well he communicates. He really wants to, you know."

I shuddered when I picked up the tape transcription of the next class session. How I had pontificated, I thought. It was as if I were daring them to communicate with me. Where was the real me in all that verbiage? Hiding behind "all deaf people?" The only identified voice was mine.

HOLLY

Now, I'm going to do something right now that I have always wanted to do. I am going to impose my conditions of communication on this group. I'm asking you to face me when you talk and don't put your hands over your mouth. I am asking you to articulate well and talk slowly. I'm also asking you: what right do I have to impose these conditions on you as a member of your group?

MAN'S VOICE

I have a very positive reaction to that. I think you have every right to say it, otherwise we aren't allowing you to be a member of this group.

HOLLY

Most people think you have to talk loud when you communicate with a deaf person. But that often increases the distortion. The most important thing is to face the person and enunciate well.

WOMAN'S VOICE

I think it would help if you reminded us of what you want us to remember. I forget sometimes to face you and speak clearly.

HOLLY

I think the biggest problem is the psychological barrier. The hearing person is afraid the deaf person isn't going to hear what he says, so he just doesn't communicate, and the deaf person sets up a psychological barrier, too.

MAN'S VOICE

I think I've mentioned this before. It was several classes before I realized you had a hearing problem. There was just no indication, or maybe I just wasn't aware of the fact that you had to look a great deal more than other people do. But you covered it up so well, or perhaps disguised it so well, that I didn't know until fairly recently that you had this problem. I think it's a good thing for you to remind us occasionally that you want us to speak directly to you so you can hear what we have to say. Otherwise, I'll forget again because you read lips so well.

HOLLY
Perhaps I read lips well because I am adventitously deaf, that is, I learned language before I lost my hearing. With the congenitally deaf it's a different problem because they are trying to lip-read a language they have never heard.

WOMAN'S VOICE
I have a question. How are you going to use this tape? Can you hear it?

HOLLY (laughing)
I have never discovered a way to lip-read a tape! I will get someone to transcribe it, and then I will read it.

WOMAN'S VOICE
I really wish you would participate more. I think you would have a lot to give.

HOLLY
Deafness is a hang-up because it imposes problems on hearing people, too. It's also an invisible handicap, one that is not apparent until you start communicating.

MAN'S VOICE
I think the whole thing we're getting at is to understand. I've been trying to look at you every time you talk to watch your lips. I don't think I would know what you were saying if I couldn't hear your voice, so I appreciate your problem. Whether you want to talk a lot or not, you are still a member of this group.

HOLLY

Only about forty percent of the English language is visible on the lips. The rest of it you have to guess, or read the expression. We have two more minutes left on the tape.

MAN'S VOICE

We appreciate yours. I like to hear you talk, because I value very much what you have to say.

HOLLY

Very few people are completely deaf. I can hear low tones, but the speech I hear is very distorted because the high frequencies are cut off. If you people didn't make any sound at all, just moved your lips, I would have a much more difficult time understanding what you have to say.

WOMAN'S VOICE

Do people with low voices come through much better than those with high voices?

HOLLY

Not necessarily, because the human voice is not pure tone. Speech is mixed frequencies. If you were to sing a song and pitch it low enough, I would hear the tune, not the...(tape runs out).

....

I put down the transcription and started to cry. I remembered now why I had felt afraid when I picked up the tape transcription. I had not heard most of the responses and was afraid I might have responded inappropriately. The members of my group had reached out and reached out and I had simply continued my intellectual discourse on deafness. Barriers, barriers, I wept. I had begged them to take theirs down and couldn't dismantle my own. They were asking to be close and I was pushing them away. I might as well have stood up in that group and said it aloud: "Don't be close!"

ten

How to Succeed in College Without Really Hearing

My first published paper appeared when I was in graduate school as I was just beginning my second year of graduate study. I was handling school better and decided, on a lark, to "pass along my experiences" gained mostly through trial and error. *The Volta Review* was a publication of the Alexander Graham Bell Association for the Deaf, and the contents are directed to deaf readers. I was shocked and pleased when they accepted it.

....

Have a hang-up about going to college? Most people do! I went through it with my three hearing sons, and although I must admit their problems were somewhat different than mine, still they were very real to them. A year and a half ago I went back to college after 27 years out of the classroom. My deafness occurred rather precipitously when I was a junior at the College of the Pacific, majoring in music, of all things. I hung on grimly until I got the degree, but I wish I had known then what I know now. Maybe it will help if I pass along some of my experiences.

In the first place, guts, if you'll excuse the expression, are more important than brains. Brains help, of course, but let's just assume that you are somewhat better than average in your reading and writing ability and you have a strong motivation to go on to college, come what may. Read on!

Check your Rehab Agency first. They have all sorts of help, including moral and (budget permitting) financial support. They also have ways of helping you decide whether you are really college material, and they find your deafness a challenge. Very refreshing.

Now, you know as well as I do that communication (for us) can only be on a one-for-one basis, and even that leaves something to be desired. But did you ever stop to think that communication is more than sound? Have you ever really assessed that psychological barrier that goes up when the hearing person suddenly realizes that you are deaf? Do you realize how much your attitude is responsible for that barrier?

Get Carl Rogers out of the library and see what he says about congruence. Listening is an art, and, believe it or not, you can learn to listen. It involves putting yourself in the other person's frame of reference. It involves assuming the other person really wants you to hear what he has to say. Quit worrying about words, words, and words. You're a lot less likely to get them if you worry about it. We really communicate by feeling and empathy. Let me give you an example.

I thought I had met my Waterloo in a seminar called Group Process in Counseling. I was straining so hard to "hear" what was going on in that group that all those units of energy the brain needs to translate "words" were being used up by stress. But I had a very wise teacher. "Forget the words, Holly," she said. "Your assignment is to chart your empathic reaction to the evolution of the group as a whole, and your feeling about the individuals in the group—not by what they say, but by how they say it."

And you know, it worked. I didn't get hung up on words. This is what Theodore Reik calls "listening with the third ear."

But on to more practical matters. You will need notetakers, at least one, possibly two, in each class. And you don't have to make a big thing out of this. At the first session of the class (which is usually orientation) there comes a pause at the end of the period and you can be sure the professor is saying "any questions?" Your hand goes up, and you explain to the professor (and the class) that you are a lip reader and because of that you always carry carbon paper with you.

Since it is impossible to read lips and write at the same time, you would appreciate any volunteers for carbon copies of their notes. Of course, there is the danger that someone very social minded (but rather stupid) would volunteer, so you may want to get more than one. But quite frankly, it doesn't really make that much difference. Professors (God bless 'em) usually mix quite a bit of redundancy with those pearls of wisdom they drop from time to time. The really important things in these notes are such things as when the next quiz is scheduled, what body of knowledge it will include, and when the next paper is due. You get most of your information from the textbook and from conferences with the professor (or teaching assistant). That's why they schedule office hours. That's what teaching is all about.

Don't wear your deafness like a defensive armor. How good you are at lip reading doesn't really make that much difference. Even the best of us miss an awful lot! But when you say "I am deaf," the natural reaction of a hearing person is to get up close, talk loud, and spit all over you. When you say, "I am a lip reader," they will be terribly intrigued. They will try to face you when they talk as well as make valiant attempts to enunciate well. That, of course, is what we want. But don't put them on the defensive. After all, it's our problem, not theirs.

Avoid beards if you can. A little difficult in this day and age, especially if you happen to be in educational psychology, as I am. However, I have been pretty lucky so far. I decided to risk it once (I had no choice) only to find that the professor had shaved off his beard between semesters and he didn't even know that I was going to be in his class. But for goodness sake, don't ask him to shave off his beard. Why he wears a beard is his problem, not yours.

Have you thought about supplementing with a correspondence course? Check with your advisor on that. It's an excellent way for a deaf person to master a subject because those correspondence courses really pour it on. Sometimes colleges transfer credits directly, but there is usually a pretty firm policy on how many units you can take and from what college. My particular college allows 24 units of credit by examination in the undergraduate division and 5 units in the graduate school. You simply take the correspondence course and then take the examination on campus. The biggest disadvantage is that invisible professor. However, there is space on the cover of each lesson that is devoted to "remarks to the professor." That is the place to "humanize" your professor. It was most successful for me in a course in Abnormal Psychology that I took by correspondence from the University of Iowa. I had the feeling that the professor and I were good friends by the time the course was finished.

There will be times when you feel that all those hours in the classroom when you can't hear what's going on is a terrible waste of time and terribly frustrating. But it's part of the game. Sit next to your notetaker and "peek." Volunteer information when your notetaker has established the topic. Who cares if someone else has already said it? It gives you a real feeling of participation.

Don't just read your notetaker's notes. Copy them into your own notebook every day, not just before the quiz. Keep current. And read, read. I usually outline the assignment before class. In that way, what is being discussed is usually something I already know. My classmates tend to think I hear more than I actually do—and if I make a "boo-boo" they very kindly do not tell me so.

Don't feel sorry for yourself. The guy sitting next to you who had a "bad trip" last night is probably worse off than you are. Above all, relax. And here are a few of Dr. James Coleman's quotes for you to think about. He authored my textbook on Abnormal Psychology (Coleman, James C., *Abnormal Psychology and Modern Life*, third edition: Scott Foresman and Co., 1964).

"Under severe stress there is a narrowing of the perceptual field and an increased rigidity of the cognitive process (page 9).

"People with a high level of anxiety tend to be rigid and inflexible and approach new problems in a stereotyped way (page 93).

"The severity of a given stress depends to a large extent on the individual's evaluation of it (page 113)."

Dr. Coleman wasn't even talking about deafness, but it fits, doesn't it?

And then, every once in a while, something very nice happens. I was trying to schedule a conference with my very busy advisor, and I caught him "on the run." "When can I see you?" I said. "I have to get my schedule straightened out before you leave." (He was going on sabbatical.)

"I don't have a free moment this week, Holly," he frowned over his appointment book. "I'll tell you what. I'll be in the office Wednesday morning. You can phone me and I'll pull your card and we'll settle it on the phone." I looked at him and grinned. "You know what?" he said softly. "I forgot."

I felt like one of the guys. I got the appointment, too.

eleven

In the Real Essence of Life
We Are Alone

The last semester at State, before I started my fieldwork, wasn't documented in my folder. I recalled that was the semester I took the course in Group Counseling I mentioned in my article; my stress level had been high as I strained for the words. No one took notes in a group-counseling situation, so I felt I should do without a notetaker. In other classes it had been easy to follow my own advice. I never lacked for volunteers, and sometimes had more than one notetaker.

....

That was also the instructor who suggested that I forget the words. "Your assignment, Holly," she said, "is to chart your empathic reaction to the group." So gradually the Listener became the Observer. Many of my classmates were warm and caring people, but I found it difficult to become fully engaged. I rented a house near the campus and took in a couple of student roomers, feeling that it was probably not good for me to live alone. I began to seek out experiences where I could be on the periphery—anonymous—and observe. As I tried to recall the significance of that period, I suddenly remembered that it was that fall, on November 16, 1969, almost a year after Jim had died, that I marched in the Moratorium Day Parade.

....

I wanted to identify with the Vietnam War protests. The first storm of the season was raging, but it seemed to enhance the symbolism, at least for me. The wind and the rain were a challenge. I was dressed warmly in ski pants, Jim's parka and overshoes, and stayed surprisingly dry underneath although the rain formed headwaters on my kerchiefed head and the rivulets that coursed my face found their way down my neck. It was a fifteen-block walk to the assembly place, and I kept emptying my pockets of rain.

There must have been a thousand people already assembled at the park when I arrived. All the beards in the county must have been there. The beards seemed to accentuate the eyes—kindly eyes, concerned eyes. For an hour they kept coming. Nine out of ten, I guessed, were college students, although there were a few families with small boys, slickered in yellow rain coats. I saw only one other woman who might have been the mother of draft-age sons; there must have been others. But when you are a part of a massive crowd, you see only those in your immediate vicinity. I saw no one I knew.

I didn't talk, though many did. The march was heavily monitored and very orderly. I saw no placards at the assembly point, only peace signs everywhere, on the back of raincoats, as armbands, on hats and umbrellas. We marched ten abreast, arms linked.

But there was a banner. Directly behind me marched the Veterans Against the War, their banner stretched between two standard-bearers. The paint on the banner was water-soluble and their sign became illegible as the rain dissolved the red paint, encroaching on the background and dripping, like blood, on the street below.

Halfway down the boulevard some Chicano families joined us, all carrying placards on standards, some in English, some in Spanish. They added a note of color and gaiety to an otherwise somber march.

Many on the roadways joined the march and swelled our numbers. We flashed peace signs to watchers on the route. Those in the windows of the high-rise office buildings seemed embarrassed; few flashed the sign back. Nestled among the massive office buildings was an old Victorian mansion, a holdout against the surrounding concrete and steel. The dining room chandelier twinkled through the rain. We flashed the peace sign and the drapes abruptly closed.

There was singing as we came to a halt on the Capitol steps. "All we are saying—is give peace a chance." One of the U.S. Senators spoke. His talk was punctuated with applause and the people seemed chagrined when they realized they could not applaud and flash the peace sign at the same time. The Senator's oratory rose and fell, and the applause followed accordingly. I didn't know what he was saying, of course, but it didn't really matter. I was very absorbed observing my fellow protesters. An old man, who must have been in his nineties, was shaking the peace sign throughout the whole address. "Good for you, old man," I thought. "You are young." A few feet in front of me, flanked by flags and torches, a young man was reading from what appeared to be a script. His words were inaudible to me, and he seemed oblivious to the crowd around him. I was momentarily puzzled. Then, "of course," I thought. "He is reading the list of war dead." It was started on Monday night and there were several pages left in the list. Another young man with an equally impassive face soon replaced him.

Quite suddenly I felt apart from the crowd. My feeling was deeply personal and I didn't want to share it. As I edged through the people, the rivulets pouring down my face tasted salty. Tears for humanity and myself? A deep sense of isolation engulfed me as I trudged to the bus stop. I had abandoned my useless scarf and my hair was plastered to my head from the rain. I stepped back in the bus shelter and lit a cigarette. As I dragged on my cigarette, a man ducked into the sanctuary from the rain and began the classic come-on.

"I don't seem to have a match," he said, patting his pockets. Wordlessly, I handed him my matches. He was well dressed, fiftyish, I supposed. He looked at me rather critically over the flame. As he handed back the matches, he said: "May I buy you a beer?"

Through my utter exhaustion, a wave of hysteria began to rise. Why Holly, you're getting picked up! "No thank you," I said softly. "I'm waiting for a bus."

"You can take a later bus."

"No," I said. "I'm very tired. I've been marching in the peace parade for the last four hours. I want to go home."

"Do you really believe that stuff?"

"Oh yes. I do indeed."

Then he started to talk. I couldn't hear much of what he said, could only watch his face, and the light was poor. I guessed he was telling me his views of the war but I really didn't know. I didn't have to know, really, any more than I had to know what the bearded ones were saying or what the Senator was orating about. For I already knew. They were all saying the same thing: "Listen to me! I am saying something I feel very deeply about. Won't you listen to me?"

So I "listened," until his monologue was interrupted by the arrival of my bus. He bowed me courteously to the door. I sank to the seat, off my feet for the first time in four hours. As I leaned my head wearily against the window, I saw my erstwhile friend, weaving up the sidewalk. He had kept his inebriation well under control while he was talking to me, but it was very evident now. No, my friend, that's not the answer either. I tried that for a while too, and it doesn't work.

What are the guises of loneliness? Enough alcohol for the courage to pick up some companionship? Pervasive guilt about a current life style? Compulsive time-filling and bravado? And underneath a deeply felt need: someone to say softly: "I know. I hear you."

I was shaking with cold and fatigue when I opened the front door. Thank God a light is on, I thought. Thank God I'm alone. I drew a hot tub and stripped off my wet clothes. Half an hour later I made a cup of cocoa and laced it liberally with rum. In the real essence of life we are alone, I thought. Oh, we stave it off as long as we can. We identify with the protesters; we applaud the speech we did not hear, we "listen" sympathetically to the lonely drunk. But it is only when we are alone that we really feel the essence of being, that we really come to terms with life. If we ever do. That night I did.

....

Now I sat at my desk for a long time in a reverie. What's the feeling, Holly? Where are you now? Four years ago, at the march, I needed to mourn Jim's passing and claim my own place—alone. Perhaps now I needed to get in touch with those feelings again. They were feelings that needed to resurface, to be experienced once more. Perhaps it was a necessary bridge between mourning and reaching out.

twelve

Therapist-Status-Not-Coded

Finally I looked down on my desk again. The remaining
documents in my folder were all related to my move from the classroom into
the workplace. Four years of therapist-in-training to get where I am now. I was
fortunate. The circumstances were right.

During the last year of classes before I started my fieldwork, I gave considerable thought to my future. The literature on deafness had fascinated me, and
the more I read, the more I realized that the really significant work was being
done with young deaf children and their families. If counseling was to be my
field, couldn't it be habilitation rather than rehabilitation? I needed to decide
soon, as what I did for my fieldwork would largely determine the path I would
take. I could postpone that decision if I went for a Ph.D., I thought. The idea
rather appealed to me, and I applied to an eastern university, motivated, perhaps,
by a desire to become another "Doctor Elliott." I also had visited an outpatient
clinic that specialized in family therapy with deaf people. There was a possibility
that I could do my fieldwork there. The clinic was affiliated with a medical
school and the psychiatrist in charge of the special project for deaf people had

expressed interest in the idea of training a deaf person as a psychotherapist. The decision seemed to rest on space; there was simply no room for another therapist. But I was drawn to the set-up and gambled that they would make room. I arranged with the eastern university to delay entrance into the Ph.D. program until I had completed my field training at the deaf clinic. At the last minute, one of the psychiatric social workers went on maternity leave, so I was in.

When I started my training period at the clinic I was considerably in awe, but I liked being back in the medical school atmosphere. Watching the young interns and residents was a link to the past, reminiscent of Jim's internship and residency half a lifetime ago. But were we ever that young? I wondered. The deaf clinic was somewhat out of the mainstream, in a converted residence a block away from the medical school, and I had little direct contact with the hospital personnel, but I enjoyed being in the periphery, observing the concerned young men and women in the cafeteria, the library, hurrying on their appointed rounds.

....

The kitchen in our building was converted into a playroom, well stocked with the diagnostic and therapeutic tools of play therapy: paints, blocks, dart guns, tool kits, doctor kits, doll houses, and toy people. I developed a fond attachment to Bobo the Clown, the inflated, resilient, child-sized doll that could take quite a beating and always bobbed upright, his smile intact. At my request, the video-tape technician became the "surgical consultant" for Bobo, on call with his kit of strong glue and plastic patches, and helpful for inflationary purposes. Occasionally Bobo "died" or became "very sick" during play therapy and at times I had to risk hyperventilation and blow him up myself, but only when all other recovery methods failed.

My office had probably been a dressing room in its previous incarnation; it was upstairs in the rear, and its only entrance and exit was through the supervisor's office. This posed something of a problem for the busy secretaries when they had a message for me. Normally, they used the buzzer and intercom, but for me they had to use their legs. Sometime later, when the staff expanded, the clinic moved to larger quarters around the block and the secretaries (those sterling characters!) insisted that my office be close to them so they would not have to run their legs off bringing me phone messages, or telling me that my patient had arrived. Consequently, I acquired a choice front office, with a fireplace.

My supervisor was a skilled psychiatric social worker who became my mentor, my telephone intermediary, and my ever-present-help-in-time-of-trouble. We had no precedents to go by, as deaf therapists were a rarity. It occurred to me that the supervisors of deaf therapists probably must spend more time with the supervisee than is usually the case. A great deal of telephone time is put to therapeutic uses, and third party intervention on a sensitive phone call is tricky at best, dealing, as often happens, with subtle responses to nuances in tone and auditory affect. During my time with her the supervisor and I developed what almost amounted to a "symbiotic telephone relationship." She was not only familiar with my cases, but also with my particular approach to problems (when I became experienced enough to have an approach). She became adept at cradling the phone between ear and shoulder, leaving her hands free to translate into sign language what the worried, and sometimes angry mother (or consultee) was saying on the other end of the line. Her expressive face also reflected the affect of the person with whom I was talking. I marveled at the empathic way she handled this. I tried to limit outgoing calls to the supervisory hour, or write letters, as many of my patients didn't use the phone either. But occasionally a secretary would appear at the door and say, "There's a phone call for you. The supervisor wants you in her office."

Most of the referrals to the clinic, I learned, were families with young deaf children, although referrals from rehab, community mental health centers and even self-referred deaf adults were seen.

My first two cases were young deaf women, both of whom transferred to me from the social worker on maternity leave. Both patients showed considerable evidence of psychopathology; one a possible "conversion reaction" (or "hysterical" deafness), the other a dynamic and dramatic young Black woman, whom I was to continue seeing on a regular basis for almost four years. We went through a great deal together, hospitalization for psychotic break, and post-hospitalization care during which I found myself, somewhat inadvertently (but also quite fortuitously) in consultation with a voodoo expert. My patient's dramatic improvement sent me back to my textbooks, searching for parallels.

It was like another world, this abrupt transition to "professionalism." I had a lot of help from the psychiatrist and the supervisor; it was a step-by-step process of acquiring a new language (signs), learning about the causes and treatment of dysfunctional behavior, and learning about deafness as a developmental disability. The supervisor worked with me on psychiatric studies of two family therapy cases, then launched me on my own, albeit with close supervision. I found I needed to read a lot between cases, to keep a jump ahead of my patients.

Toward the end of my training period, the psychiatrist asked me to remain on the staff. If that was to be my decision, I needed to let the eastern university know, as I had already been awarded a generous grant to study for the Ph.D. There followed a few days of lonely decision-making. I wanted to discuss it with my family, but the boys all lived out of the state and I could not phone them. I sensed Jim saying: "Gut-level psychotherapy, Holly. Why do you want a Ph.D.?" The psychiatrist said: "I want to train you as a psychotherapist. We need you here." I decided to stay.

After I was appointed to the clinical staff there was some discussion about what to call me. I was doing psychiatric social work, but that was not my degree. I was on the university salary schedule as a vocational rehabilitation counselor, but that was not what I was doing. The psychiatrist came up with the title "counselor-therapist" and so it remained. The computer in medical records called me "therapist-status-not-coded," and that was okay, too.

And my "life history" folder continued to grow: the write-up of a conference with the mother of a deaf child, copy of a talk I had given on play therapy with deaf children, a letter from the father of a deaf child, an article about a deaf child written for a deaf periodical, a newspaper clipping.

I was soon caught up in the oral-manual controversy: should a deaf child learn speech and speech reading only, or should sign language be added, too? Some of my hearing parents strongly believed in one method; some were equally convinced that the other way was right. Deaf parents did not see this as a problem; they simply taught signs to their deaf and hearing children alike. I was having hang ups of my own with sign language. With some people I was fairly fluent; with others I stammered on my hands.

When I started my professional career, my own identity crisis had not been resolved.

thirteen
Total Communication

During my training period (and later) the psychiatrist occasionally invited me to sit in on a conference with the mother of a deaf child. The psychiatrist had a marvelous way with these troubled parents and I could usually pick up the feeling, if not all of the words. Initially, I felt that I should also contribute something to these sessions; after all, I was deaf myself and perhaps I Had Something Important to Say. The psychiatrist had told me, after one such session, that I talked too much, that my role in these conferences was to observe and listen. I had retreated quickly after that, feeling somewhat victimized. Thinking about it later, it occurred to me that the experience had been "a necessary turning point," something I needed to hear to counter my tendency to intellectualize about the condition of deafness, which had been, in all probability, a defensive stance, or even a form of resistance to the "deaf condition." As I tried to get in touch with that feeling again, I wondered if I had been unconsciously setting myself up as a "victim" expecting to be rejected, which was not the psychiatrist's intent at all. What was that graffiti I had seen on a building near the bus stop? "Criticism is a form of love." I didn't understand that then. But my "victim" role was getting uncomfortable and I chuckled to myself as I recalled my uncharacteristic outburst at a staff meeting shortly after I had been officially appointed to the clinical staff.

When the psychiatrist wanted my attention during staff meeting she had rapped sharply on the table. This always brought not only me to attention, but everyone else as well. I had tried to rationalize it, saying to myself that it certainly was a good way to get my attention; that, after all, I was deaf and would have to learn to put up with these little indignities (victim, victim!). But it continued to bother me. Finally, brought sharply to attention once too often, I banged the table in reply. "I wish you'd stop doing that," I said to the startled psychiatrist. "It bugs hell out of me." She immediately picked up a prescription pad and wrote: "I will never pound the table again!" and gave it to me. The psychiatrist told me later that she had been enormously reassured by my expression of anger, and was delighted to see it come out. And she never pounded the table again, I realized. Instead she sort of gyrated like a windmill, which delighted me.

The clinic was one of the first in the country to advocate "total communication" in dealing with deaf children particularly. That is, we counseled using the total range of communication simultaneously—sign language, lip reading, trained vocalization. My part in this whole program involved pretty intense feelings, and I struggled to get out from under the "deaf condition" and relate at a more personal level. "Deafness" was what it was all about at the clinic, and since most of the staff members (including me) were less than fluent in sign language, a mutual decision had been made whereby everyone would use speech and signs when communicating with me. The practice could only be beneficial and in the long run, I would understand more. I knew I had hang-ups; fitting the conversation to the known sign vocabulary was often cumbersome, slow, and lacked spontaneity.

"I need (what's the sign for 'information'? I supply the sign) information about (what's the sign for 'tendency'? I supply the sign) tendency …and so on. I had been acutely aware that, imperceptibly, they began assuming that I could not understand unless they signed. This was often true in a group situation such as staff meeting. It was also true that sometimes at staff meetings signing became too frustrating or slow, or some key person did not know sign language. I really preferred looking at the person who was talking to pick up the feeling. But are feelings more important than words? Once in a while, when time was short and information crucial, I would remind the staff member that I could understand speech on a one-for-one basis, but on a couple of occasions the staff member shared her frustration with signs, and never signed with me again. And, in a way, this defeated the purpose: signs are important, "deafness" is what it's all about at the clinic, staff members need to be more comfortable with signs, and I could understand better if they used both speech and signs. Sometimes my role as designated guinea pig weighed heavily on me. I sighed. Although in the long run the "experiment" had increased the fluency of almost everyone's signs (including mine), it was still a dilemma I took a long time resolving to my satisfaction.

It must be remembered, that I was one of the first deaf people to become a professional therapist. Staff was learning with me, too. Today, sign language interpreters are added to the staff; computer-assisted notetaking transfers the spoken word into text. The problem today is: which sign language? Signed English or ASL (American Sign Language)?

I became more comfortable, however, in my role as observer when I was invited to sit in with the psychiatrist at a parent conference. Occasionally I would share an observation of my own when I felt it was appropriate. I remember taking notes at one such conference, making a point of transcribing them later. They had been difficult to read, as the process of lip reading and writing at the same time left something to be desired as far as legibility was concerned. I drew the transcription from my folder and smiled when I realized that my own imagination had created something that may not have been faithful to what had actually transpired. But I was pleased with the result: The conference included many points that had helped me in my own work with troubled parents and that was what good teaching was all about.

....

Mrs. Clark was anxious when she came in, under rather tight control. She was an intelligent; middle-class woman, and she obviously took her child-rearing seriously. Her face reflected the despair she felt, but anger was there, too. She had invested so much in Robert, with (to her) so little results. Her anger was also, one suspects, being projected on Robert's teacher, as he was regressing in school. He was a bright lad, eight years old, and he had previously shown good potential for speech, but in the last few weeks refused to talk spontaneously.

Mrs. Clark began talking about the summer program at Robert's school. "They have a good program in our area," she said. "Robert will be going to summer school every morning. They will concentrate on speech and language, and for one full day each week they will go on a field trip and put that language to use. Robert's primary problem now is speech. He doesn't use language until you ask him to. He used to, but he doesn't now."

The psychiatrist wondered if Robert thought that language was something that mother wanted. "Some schools force it, parents force it, special classes force it."

"Perhaps the fun is taken out of it," Mrs. Clark said.

"It's no fun to use language if it's a chore."

"But the teacher has a rigid manner," Mrs. Clark continued. "She is very structured. She has a discipline problem in the classroom. She thinks Robert is brain damaged and this upsets me. She doesn't believe me when I tell her that he is bright. Personally, I think he's bored."

"That happens," said the psychiatrist. "Bright kids can pretend they are stupid when the teacher expects it."

Mrs. Clark became more agitated. "If they're not firm with him at school, I have to do it. But when I try to stimulate language by using a book, he just wants to turn the pages. He gives excuses. I have helped him with math—filling in the blanks for consecutive numbers—and he can do this very rapidly when he wants to. The teacher doesn't understand many of his words and if the teacher doesn't ask for language, he's not going to use it. It's very discouraging. We've lost another year."

"Have you been getting counseling yourself?" asked the psychiatrist.

"Yes. I can cope better with Robert now. He seems to be happier."

"Because you're happier?"

"That may be why. But Robert has got to get reading. When they talk about 'total communication' they should include reading."

"When you refer to 'total communication' what did you mean?"

"Well, we're raising Robert for a hearing world, and feel that he should be as 'oral' as possible. We want him to be able to communicate by speech and speech reading. He did beautifully for a while, but he isn't retaining what he learned."

"You know," said the psychiatrist after a brief pause, "some deaf kids get so much pressure to talk that they clam up. I wonder how often they stop because they've 'had it up to here.'"

"He's been given all sorts of opportunities to use speech and language."

"Including table pounding?" the therapist asked.

"'Well yes, it started that way. He started wearing a hearing aid when he was twenty-two months old. He likes it okay, but often he has to be reminded to put it on."

"Do both you and your husband feel the same way about speech and language?"

"Well, my husband is more difficult to lip read than I am and I understand more of Robert's words."

"You do speak clearly," the psychiatrist interjected. "You may have noticed that I have not asked you to repeat."

Mrs. Clark looked pleased.

"Do you know many deaf adults?" the psychiatrist continued.

"A few," replied Mrs. Clark. "We talked to one who paid a great deal of attention to Robert and Robert really enjoyed it. He said to Robert: 'You can't hear. I can't hear either.' Robert seemed quite surprised. We only saw him once, but it was a good experience."

"It's important for deaf kids to know that that deaf people grow up, too. It's also important for parents. When did Robert have his last audiogram?"

"About a year ago. It had improved a lot over the audiogram he had when he was smaller."

"Early audiograms are not always reliable," said the psychiatrist. "Sometimes children want to fight it."

"Yes, that was true when he was younger," Mrs. Clark said. "It's better now. His hearing is better in the lower frequencies, too. We can be very firm with him now when he has an audiogram."

"Do you think you feel less comfortable being firm with him because of the deafness?" the psychiatrist asked.

"I have always been firm with him. We did make many mistakes in the beginning. When he would have an argument with his older sister I would finally say 'Oh Marian, give it to him.' I know that was the easy way out. I am much more firm with him now."

There was a short silence, broken by the psychiatrist. "Language can be used as a weapon," she finally said. "Deaf kids get fed up and their attitude about speech becomes a tight-mouthed 'make me.' I wonder if that's what is happening to Robert now." Mrs. Clark made no comment.

"You know," the psychiatrist continued, "I'm in something of a quandary. I don't know Robert and I have the feeling that you may think we brainwash people about manual communication. Some youngsters take speech therapy well; sometimes speech therapy accomplishes just the opposite, and something else needs to be done."

"But he loves to look at books," said Mrs. Clark. "It's just that he's not interested in learning the sequence of words—he wants to turn the page. If we could just get across to him that the words are important."

"How can you accomplish that?"

"If he's interested in the pictures wouldn't it naturally follow that he'd want to find out more about the pictures by getting to know the words?"

"I wonder," mused the psychiatrist, "I wonder if we might show you our linguistic videotapes. We are doing some research on very young deaf children who are learning signs, speech, and speech reading simultaneously. We find that signs and finger spelling reinforce speech and as speech improves, signs lessen. Would you like to see the videotapes?"

"Well, I don't know," Mrs. Clark hesitated. "We want him to be oral."

"Sometimes if a child is permitted to use sign language, he will talk more."

"I agree in principle," Mrs. Clark said. "But with Robert, he is so bright and has a tendency to take the easy way out. I am afraid if he uses signs his speech would deteriorate."

"Holly has a case," said the psychiatrist, gesturing to me.

"Yes," I said. "This youngster had many pressures and a great deal of tutoring in speech in her early years. Her teacher introduced sign language this year and we made a videotape of her response when I told her I had talked with her teacher, who told me she was learning signs. This seemed to remove an emotional block and her communication in all modes improved dramatically. It seemed to make language a fun thing."

"And now you don't have fun," said the psychiatrist, "and Robert doesn't have any fun either."

But Mrs. Clark was still set in worry lines. "He knows I want him to learn language," she said. "When he doesn't use a whole sentence such as 'give me…a…cookie,' I tell him I don't understand him."

"Do you?" asked the psychiatrist.

"Do I what?"

"Understand him?"

"Yes, of course, but I want to get him to say the whole sentence."

"Maybe it's confusing to him when you say 'I don't understand you.' Sort of like fibbing. Why don't you say 'I don't like it,' which is true?

"I never thought of that," said Mrs. Clark, with a laugh. Then more tentatively, "I don't know if sign language would reduce tensions or not."

"It wouldn't, unless you were comfortable using it."

Mrs. Clark sighed. "We have talked about it, my husband and I. We recognize it as something Robert will want to learn later. But we feel he should be oral as long as possible. If we could just get him over the hump where he wants to talk."

"I certainly respect your opinion," the psychiatrist said.

"I've learned to sign," I said, "but I'm certainly in favor of speech and speech reading. It's very important to me."

"I am afraid," Mrs. Clark resumed, "that if he starts sign language he will get past the point of adapting to speech."

"What makes you think that is true?" the psychiatrist asked.

"Well, if he concentrates on looking at the hands he won't look at the lips, and that bothers me. He had such wonderful success earlier in the oral method. I really feel that his teacher is responsible for his regressing. She just doesn't encourage language."

"Would it help if we arranged a conference with the teacher?"

Mrs. Clark didn't reply directly. "Parents are supposed to help children, too, but they need cooperation from the teacher. I don't know about sign language…I could be wrong."

"I know it's a tough decision to make," said the psychiatrist sympathetically. "If I had any inkling that signs would inhibit speech, I would feel differently than I do. But it's been our experience here that when a child is allowed to sign, his speech improves. Of course, speech has to be encouraged at the same time. It's not an either/or situation; it's both."

Mrs. Clark looked tearful. "I'm willing to try anything that will help Robert."

"If you feel that sign language might help," the psychiatrist said gently, "it will only if you choose to do it, too. It probably wouldn't help if it became a chore for Robert."

"My husband is willing to try anything, too."

"We have a speech therapist here that works with some of our patients. She uses a combination of speech, speech reading, finger spelling, and signs."

Mrs. Clark sighed again. "Last year they started a new class at Robert's school using the simultaneous approach. These were children who could not learn speech and speech reading. It was organized last year."

"We feel that sign language should not be used as a last resort," the psychiatrist said firmly. "If the children have been labeled as failures, then both they and the parents fight sign language. If I had a deaf child, I would start sign language and speech at about six months of age. Were the children in this class considered retarded?'

"They were not making progress," said Mrs. Clark. "I don't know why they were offered total communication. But I'm very concerned about what will happen to Robert in the fall. The special classes integrate with the hearing classes as much as possible. Robert would be better integrated with children his own age, as he is big for his age. And he did poorly at his grade level last year and maybe he should repeat the grade. I don't know what to expect. I feel that reading and math should be given the first thing in the morning when the children are fresh, but the teacher feels they should get speech and language first. Which should it be?"

"That is always a problem," the psychiatrist replied. "Experts say this is the way to go but experts disagree and everyone becomes dissatisfied. Everyone wants to find ways to bring deaf children to grade level and there are many different methods out there."

"Robert is behind grade level now, particularly in speech and language. But he does seem happier now."

"Happy children can be academically behind. Why don't you talk it over with your husband and let me know if you would like me to have a conference with the teacher. In the meantime, we'll talk to our on-staff speech therapist about the possibility of speech therapy here. You can get in touch with us about that. And, we're always available to you and your husband if you want to talk again."

Mrs. Clark sighed again, but this time it seemed to be with relief. "I'd really appreciate that. It was helpful to talk about this today. It has always been something I've sort of skirted around; something we didn't really want to face. Perhaps it's all tied up with the feeling that deep inside we have a hard time accepting the fact that Robert is deaf. It's pretty overwhelming, really."

"I know," the psychiatrist said gently. "But he really is deaf, isn't he?"

"Yes," said Mrs. Clark. "He is deaf. He is, indeed."

fourteen

Try Listening to Rock
When All You Can Hear Is
the Bass

I had been on the staff for less than a month when I
received an extraordinary letter from the father of a deaf child. Mr. Phillips had
read a short biography of me in the registry of an organization that promoted
"oral" education of deaf children and was generally opposed to signs. He
wondered how it was possible for a profoundly deaf person to have majored in
music and directed choirs. He had many questions: "How can a deaf person
direct a choir? What is your hearing loss in decibels? What kind of music did
you have in your home? Did you hear any of it? Did you have trouble finding
work? It is difficult for a hearing person with an ear for music to recognize that
a deaf parent can cultivate an interest in music in her children? What do you
have to say about that? What can you say about the effect of musical experience
on your speech? After all, music is definitely auditory training. We expose our
deaf son to music whenever we can because we know he gets something
through the vibrations. We have taught him some elementary dance (to music)
because we feel that rhythmic experience will be better for his speech. Do you
agree?"

I put down his letter and pulled out the copy of my reply. It seems longer than I remember, I thought, as I began to read. Did I tell this stranger my whole life story?

....

"Dear Mr. Phillips," I wrote. "Your astonishing and thoughtful letter has been received and deserves a thoughtful answer. I was distressed when I read that little biography you refer to, not because of what it did say, but because of what it did not say. This changes the picture.

"Most importantly, I have not always been deaf. My deafness occurred when I was nineteen in college, so my music major was a case of finishing what I had already started. Not easy, perhaps, but not certainly not impossible, as it would have been had I always been deaf, or had my deafness occurred before I started college.

"Another factor is the nature of my hearing loss. You ask me what my loss is in decibels, and I must ask: at what frequency? If you average out those frequencies (as they do in those research projects), I would tell you that my loss is around 80 decibels, which is considered profound. But if you look at my audiogram, you would see that at the frequency of 250 cycles per second the loss is 100 decibels, at 500 cps it is 50 decibels and at 1,000 cps there is nothing, or no sound at any intensity. Most speech sounds, as you probably know, fall into the 500 to 4,000 frequency range, so I retain the lower left hand corner of the speech range as the line drops precipitously from 250 to 1000 cycles per second It is what my audiologist calls 'a small island of sound,' but it is useful, indeed. It means that I can probably hear you talk, but I do not know what you are saying unless I look at you. Speech sounds are such a mixture of frequencies, and my cutoff point is very low pitched. I tend to hear vowels (which are generally lower frequencies) but no consonants (which are higher).

"Music, however, tends to be more pure tone. Therefore, I can distinguish musical sounds up to 400 cps, which is the A above middle C on the piano. These tones are not the tones that you hear, as I do not hear the overtones that add richness and depth to the music. But they are distinguishable, and this, plus my memory for music, enables me to take what I can hear and pattern the rest in my mind. Parenthetically, this may have been what happened to Beethoven, although there is evidence that his deafness was middle ear, or conductive, deafness, rather than inner ear, or nerve deafness, as mine is. Thus, Beethoven's music got progressively louder as he tried to crash the sound barrier, as witness that glorious Ninth Symphony. If today's surgical techniques and sophisticated hearing aids had been available in Beethoven's day, who knows? We might even have a Tenth, Eleventh, and Twelfth Symphony! But for me, loud music increases the distortion. And nerve deafness is not, at least not yet, amenable to surgical intervention.

"But the point is that Beethoven knew music before he became deaf, and he could imagine what it sounded like even if he had great difficulty hearing it. With my choirs, I spent very little time on intonation; I left that entirely up to the considerable talents of the members of the choir. I spent a great deal of time on expression, rhythm, and interpretation of the meaning I thought the words and music were trying to convey. My choirs usually sang *a capella*, or unaccompanied, as the organ tended to drown out what I could hear. I could hear the bass, lip read the sopranos, and I always knew if the sopranos were off pitch by the expression on the tenors' faces—and I always had very expressive tenors!

"Another advantage I have, of course, was that my language base was established before I became deaf. I have to be very careful that this does not become a problem in my present work. Occasionally, parents of deaf children will assume that because my speech is good, their child's speech can be good, too. I must often point out that my deafness is not prelingual, and maintaining the speech I already learned is quite different from learning speech that you have never heard at all.

"My husband was a physician and my entire orientation was with hearing people. Often I pretended I could hear and got away with it pretty well because my speech was good. But it was not very comfortable, that denial, and it didn't work for more than superficial situations. Occasionally the means did justify the ends. Several years ago I took a two weeks summer session in choir directing from John Finley Williamson, one of the giants in the field. He did castigate me in front of the class telling me I should do something about my speech defect (sibilants are difficult) but he never did know that I was deaf. He did tell me, at the end of the second session, that I was a 'good choir director.' It has since occurred to me that choir directing is a form of manual communication.

"In an attempt to reorganize my life a couple of years ago, I decided to go back to school and get a master's in rehabilitation counseling and work with the deaf. Since getting the degree I have changed directions somewhat and I am now on the staff of a deaf mental health clinic. I see all kinds of problems, oral and manual, and I'm learning—and using—the language of signs.

"Perhaps I am influenced by the fact that I see—and treat—some of the failures of the oral method. Yet who is to say what is failure and what is success? It certainly is not the failure of the child, but it may be the failure of society in imposing demands upon the child that cannot be met.

"This is not to say that I reject the oral approach, but it is to say that I see advantages in both. Oral skills are very important to me and without them my life would be very restricted. But restrictions, to a great extent, are something every deaf person must learn to live with, whether he is oral or manual, adventitiously or prelingually deaf. Sure, this is a hearing world, but I am not a hearing person, and although I am a good lip reader, I only get bits and pieces of what is being said, and a great deal of speech is not really visible on the lips. I am thankful for those bits and pieces, but I want more than that. Humans are social creatures, and they must communicate, and it must be in the way that is most comfortable for them and, in the case of small children, comfortable for the parents as well. The most relaxed deaf people I know are those who can talk and who can sign. I wish I knew the answers but the answers must be very, very individual. I, for one, would like to remain open to all. To my way of thinking, no language should be labeled a 'bad' language, as 'bad' is to label a child who uses that language (or cannot learn the 'accepted' language) a 'failure,' and the psychic consequences can be profound. One mother of a deaf child I know seems to be meeting this challenge. She says: 'We are teaching her our language (speech) and learning her language (signs).' Whether this child becomes oral or manual (or both, as I suspect will be the case), she will not be a 'failure.'

"The ability to learn language, the psychologists would have us believe, may be inherent, an inborn ability that the child brings to the task of language learning. What I am referring to, of course, is language, not speech. Speech is only an outward manifestation of language. Language must be internalized before it can be meaningfully expressed. Thus, some deaf children learn signs first, and then superimpose their speech upon that. The problem with many deaf children is that we get the cart before the horse.

"What the psychologists say about language may also be true about music. I come from a very musical family, but a largely untrained one, and I seem to have inherited my father's musical ability. I could improvise all over the piano keyboard, and when I went to college I wanted to learn why as well as how. The cart before the horse, indeed. My sons have had the opportunity of musical training, and they have apparently inherited the ability, as they are all musical, although music is an avocation, not a vocation, with them. The stereo always took precedence over the TV in our home and if it wasn't the stereo, it was the piano, or the trumpet, or the French horn, or the drums, or any combination thereof. But it was in their idiom, not mine. Try listening to rock when all you can hear is the bass! But their pleasure was my pleasure, particularly when they all got going at once and the house fairly shook.

"I don't think a deaf mother who had never heard music would be interested in encouraging her child in music, any more than a hearing mother would encourage her child to learn Swahili. It's simply not in her experience.

"And I struggle over your final question. What can I say, you ask, about the effect of music on my speech? I believe that music has had a profound effect on my ability to communicate, but no influence whatever on my speech. I could be wrong, but I feel that music is in an affective domain, not a cognitive one. I applaud your efforts with your son as you expose him to rhythmic experience and the feel of music. Music as a mode of expression can be very important to him, maybe even because it does not require speech. Deaf youngsters, I believe need emotional outlets for expression that are quite apart from 'talk, talk, talk.'

Some children find this outlet in temper tantrums, others in hyperactivity. Many simply withdraw. And music, I suppose, could be called auditory training, but my advice would be to forget the training aspect and offer rhythm and the feel of music for its own sake. It might even serve the purpose of relieving tensions that would interfere with the ability to learn speech—and believe me, that is important.

....

"The greatest pleasure I get from music now is singing a song in sign language. If I pitch it low enough I can still sing it while signing it. Signs are rhythmic and a beautiful accompaniment to a song; to me, this is the ultimate interpretation of music. I keep enlarging my repertoire, as I was blessed with a second alto voice. I find this enormously satisfying.

"I seem to have mounted a forum, Mr. Phillips, and perhaps I have answered more than you asked for. If so, I beg your indulgence. Thank you for writing and thank you also for listening."

As I put down the copy of my letter I realized that I had never heard from Mr. Phillips again. Well, I thought, he had asked about music, and I had jumped to my own conclusions by offering him an intellectual discourse on sign language. I talk too much, I sighed. Words will not change things, particularly if the person has invested time and effort in a different approach. Only research and results will change things. I did feel that I had made some progress since I wrote that letter, though; I felt considerably less need to be strident in defense of signs.

I could understand better by then because I was wearing a hearing aid. I had tried one before, but when the low sounds were amplified the roar was so loud it hurt and the distortion was increased. My audiologist recently had supplied me with a hearing aid that compressed sound at the lower frequencies and did not blast my head off at 250 cps. In fact, it was crafted to my audiogram, a new development in hearing aids. It did not amplify the "no response' frequencies, but within my "small island of sound" it helped. My colleagues told me that my speech improved whenever I wore the aid; that is, they could under-stand me better. I suggested that since that was the case, I would pass the hat and they could help me pay for the hearing aid, but somehow they were not very responsive to that idea.

I doubted that I could direct choirs now—my latest audiogram showed that my progressive loss was increasing at a much more rapid rate than before and soon I would probably require sign language on a one-on-one basis, too. But I still enjoyed singing in signs, particularly when I was alone, driving a car. It may have been something of a traffic hazard, but I could drive one-handed. And besides, it was fun.

fifteen

The Silent Message

Turning back to my folder, I noticed that the next batch of papers was jumbled up. At first I didn't know what they were. Ah, I thought. The talk I gave to a group of parents of deaf children. These are the process notes and case studies I consulted. At the bottom I found a working draft of the talk I gave to a group of parents of deaf children.

I remember my knees still shaking as I sat down at my desk to write up the notes on the latest confrontation with Bobby, the "Thunder Baby," as I privately called him. What had precipitated his rampage in the playroom? "And when he's madder'n mischief/ He rolls and growls and spits/ And kicks the clouds all forty ways/ And gives the weather fits." Bobby had started willingly enough into the playroom and had passed the coffee machine, then had turned back to make himself a cup of hot chocolate. Occasionally he took a cup of chocolate into the playroom with him, although it usually stayed on the sink and became cold as his attention was engaged with other things. But today the chocolate box had been empty, and I carried him kicking and screaming into the playroom, and had locked the door behind us.

Bobby was an eight-year-old rubella-syndrome child; his mother had German measles during the first three months of her pregnancy, and as a result, he was probably profoundly deaf, extremely hyperactive, and very anxious. His mother admitted in despair that she simply could not cope with him. He was well aware of this and it increased his anxiety as he continuously tested limits in an unconscious effort to get someone to stop him.

Another therapist witnessed the temper tantrum in the hall and offered assistance, but I declined, feeling that Bobby and I needed to work this out for ourselves. After I deposited him on the floor of the playroom, I sat down beside him in an attempt to relate to his anger but he would have no part of this. With great sweeping arcs of his arms he sent all the toys on the shelves crashing to the floor. He opened drawers and upended the contents into a jumbled heap on the floor.

I stood aside and watched him gravely. There appeared to be a certain method in his anger, a discharge of frustration perhaps, a certain statement about his present condition. When I could catch his eye I signed that I knew he was very angry, but the rampage continued. He was not breaking the rules. He was not hurting himself or me, and he knew that he could make a mess of the play-room as long as he helped clean it up later. I was watching carefully for cues, and was rather surprised at the calmness I felt. Bobby had picked up a block and cocked his arm as if to aim it at me, but I had held his gaze steadily and signed, "You will not hurt me." The block hit the wall and fell into the heap of toys. Finally, his energy spent, he defiantly seated himself in a corner, folded his arms, and glared.

I took a deep breath and slowly surveyed the scene. I picked up a fallen doll, placed it in a seated position on the playroom floor, sat down in front of the doll, and started a conversation.

"Well," I signed to the doll, "this playroom is really messed up." The doll, manipulated by me, nodded in agreement. "What do you think we should do about it?" I asked the doll. The doll's right palm brushed over the palm of the left hand in the "clean up" sign. In my peripheral vision I could see Bobby watching this transaction intently, but when I looked at him he quickly shifted his gaze.

"That's a good idea," I signed to the doll. "Will you help me?" The doll nodded. Then the doll walked over to the toy schoolhouse that was lying on its side, walked around it, and looked up at me.

"Well," I said pantomiming now, "this school-house is upside down on the floor. You take that end. I'll take this end, and we'll see if we can get it right side up again. Careful, it's heavy! There, that's fine. Now let's lift it up to the shelf." And (oh inspiration!) we put it away on the wrong shelf.

Bobby was out of his corner like a shot. "No!" he signed. "Not there! Here!"

"Oh?" I signed back. "Will you show us where it goes?" He stalked over to the shelf, picked up the schoolhouse and firmly deposited it in its proper place. I nodded, and stepped back, out of the way.

Then Bobby proceeded to clean up the playroom. He aligned each toy with exact precision on the shelf. He repacked the box of blocks, each fitted into its allotted space. All of the furniture went back into the dollhouse in precise order, with the doll family lined up in front of the house, beginning with the father doll and progressing down to the smallest baby doll. Teacher doll was placed behind her desk in the schoolhouse. Students were sitting at their desks, all facing the teacher. Clay went back into cans with lids firmly clamped down. He wiped off the sink with a sponge; he swept the floor. The playroom had never been so clean.

I had not intruded on the cleaning up process, but stood watching him, aware that my heart was beating fast. When the playroom was clean, Bobby stood surveying the scene for a moment or two, then looked at me—and grinned. I felt a wave of pure ecstasy flood through me and I wanted to hug him, but felt the situation called for a more mature approach. I signed to him, "The playroom looks very nice," and stuck out my hand. Bobby pumped my hand up and down. "I think it's time to stop now," I signed. Bobby nodded gravely and unlocked the door himself. As I watched his figure swagger down the hall I swore it was ten feet tall. Then my knees began to shake.

....

I looked again at my notes. What if he had been out of control completely? I wondered. What if he hadn't responded, I wondered. What would I have done then? But he did respond. He knew I trusted him. His message had been loud and clear: Let me get myself out of this hole I put myself in. I want order in my life.

The silent message. I referred to the draft of my talk. "Behavior is a form of communication particularly for a deaf child who knows few words. What is the silent message?"

When I first started doing play therapy it was difficult not to engage the child myself, to give him a joyful, happy hour to take his mind off his troubles, but I soon realized that was entertainment, not therapy. The textbooks on play therapy emphasized that the child leads the way, the therapist follows. Some of the children had difficulty with this. I thought of Carrie, child of many foster homes, who simply could not believe that she was allowed to do anything she wanted to in the playroom; she could not believe that I was not going to tell her what to do. Carrie would pick up a toy, discard it, go to something else, look at me, see something she wanted more, look at me again, drop that, and scurry around like a confused little mouse searching for a reward at the end of the maze. I wondered if Carrie ever would finish anything she started, she was such a little bundle of anxiety. Although she looked at me often, she had difficulty holding that gaze for any length of time, and it was a problem getting her to help clean up the playroom.

"Cleaning up is important, too," I told the parents. "In a therapeutic sense, the child needs to know that what we mess up we can also put back together again."

One day Carrie picked up the girl hand puppet and put it on her left hand. Suddenly her face turned vicious and with her right hand she alternated between slapping the puppet sharply on the face and signing "Bad girl, bad girl!" When this had reached a fever pitch, she suddenly threw the puppet across the room, then looked intently at me. I looked at her, then at the puppet. I pointed to the puppet on the floor. "Is she happy?" I signed to Carrie. She shook her head. My gaze went back to the puppet, then to Carrie again. "Is she sad?"

"Yes." Her fist went up and down in the sign.

"Is she crying?"

"Yes."

"Is she afraid?"

"Yes."

During this whole exchange Carrie's held my gaze steadily, and I was aware of the fast beating of my own heart, which always seemed to accompany a significant breakthrough in therapy. Carrie's eyes filled with unshed tears. My eyes were stinging too. Finally she broke the spell and imperiously ordered me to pick up the puppet. I walked across the room, picked up the puppet, patted it lovingly, and handed it back to Carrie. She calmly put the puppet to bed and the play therapy hour was over.

"Rescue me!" Carrie was saying silently. "Rescue me!"

"Intrusiveness is a problem with deaf children," I told the parents' group. "After countless hours of talking with parents of deaf children, teachers of deaf children; after watching many hours of videotapes of myself and the child in the playroom, I have become convinced that intrusiveness is a problem that is common to all emotionally disturbed deaf children. Webster defines 'intrusion' as the 'forcing of one's self in without leave or welcome.' Inadvertently we all do this with deaf children, and with the best intentions, defined often as 'what is best for the deaf child.'"

Bruce, I thought. He always locked the playroom door himself and I surmised at first specifically to keep his little sister from intruding on session. But I quickly became aware that his silent message manifested itself in other ways, too. "Please leave me alone."

The first time we were videotaped, Bruce was furious. "No!" he had shouted to me when he saw the camera on the other side of the window.

"Okay, Bruce," I signed to him, "If you don't want it, tell him to stop." I saw the playback of the tape; Bruce's angry face was glaring at the viewer as the edge of his right hand sharply hit the palm of his left hand in the sign for "stop" and for good measure he had yanked the curtain across the window, obliterating the screen. Probably the shortest videotape on record, I thought, but also one of the most explicit.

Bruce loved to play with the cars and trucks, and both he and I had sufficient residual hearing to be very much aware of the human motor that accompanied the cars as they went round and round on the playroom floor. He will wear out his vocal cords, I had thought as the "diesel" truck shifted from compound low to low to high over and over again. He did not invite me to play with him and I did not intrude, but one day the diesel overturned, and I suddenly revved up my own human motor as I brought the tow truck swiftly to the rescue. Bruce rocked back on his heels, threw back his head, and laughed aloud in pure joy. I laughed too, wishing that was on videotape. Shortly thereafter I asked him if it was okay to "take movies" again and he surprisingly agreed, possibly because he knew he could stop it if he wished—or because he felt more comfortable with himself. In his most recent videotape he had "hammed it up" for the camera, doing all sorts of silly things for the first few minutes, then settled down to play with little thought of intrusion.

Bruce had enjoyed watching the playback of the videotapes; most of the children did. I realized that watching yourself on TV could be a big ego boost for a child; one mother reported that her child cried when she could not find herself on the TV set at home. I also had a hunch that the kids were making some decisions about their own behavior as seen on the TV screen. (I knew I was making decisions about my behavior!) Their reactions to seeing themselves also gave me important clues as I attempted to structure a diagnostic formulation.

Some children were too disturbed to recognize themselves on the television screen. Bradley was one such child. Although his mother reported that he watched cartoons intently, he never gave the slightest indication that he knew himself on the TV screen. Bradley could see well enough; in fact he was very imitative, and extremely perceptive of other peoples' feelings. You could never get away with pretending with Bradley, and throughout my years of work with him, he graphically illustrated to me the importance of showing real feelings to an emotionally disturbed child. (Or any child, I quickly amended; how quickly children pick up phony adult behavior!)

....

Bradley's silent message was very clear at the beginning of one play therapy session. I talked to his mother first, and she said something that made me angry. Although I had not discharged this anger, I did think I had it under control. But when I went into the playroom, he had bitten me, deep enough to draw blood. "I know you're angry," Bradley seemed to say, "but I don't know why. So I'll give you a reason to be angry. Then I won't feel so confused."

"Does your child like himself?" I asked the parents. "That may be the most important mental health question you can ask."

Twelve-year-old David didn't like himself, and I found myself feeling uncomfortable with him because he made it very plain in the playroom that he didn't like me either. He would not engage in play, but sat in a chair signing over and over: "I don't like you. I don't like you." It was not an easy feeling to be confronted by an angry, hostile, strong, and husky youngster who seemed to want to hurt me. I had never been really afraid with David, and I knew that if I really was, he would pick that up very quickly, manipulate it, and therapy would go down the drain. But he was potentially dangerous, so I struck an agreement with the research assistant who volunteered to stay with him in the waiting room during my session with his mother. Bill was young and husky too, and had agreed to position himself outside the playroom door in case I had to call for help. Fortunately I never did, but it was comforting knowing that Bill was there.

"I don't like you," David signed again.

"That's okay," I signed back. "You don't have to like me. What I really want is for you to like yourself." He sighed, got up from his chair, and walked over to stand in front of the shelves, staring at the toys.

David's favorite toy ultimately became the rubber-tipped dart gun. Now I had problems of my own with this toy; I didn't like guns, even toy guns, pointed at me, so I had told David that he could shoot anything he wanted in that playroom, but he couldn't shoot me. I was not really been comfortable with this self-imposed rule; I realized that he needed to discharge his aggressive feelings even against me, and after all, a rubber tipped dart wouldn't really harm me—but there it was. I had established the rule. I would enforce it. On one occasion, David removed the rubber tip from the dart and pointed the gun at me, signing that he was going to shoot my eyes out. My adrenaline went up, but I advanced slowly on him with my hand out, holding his gaze. He gave up the toy, and it seemed to me that he also looked relieved.

But one time David did shoot me, so I took the dart gun away from him and put it on a high shelf. During the next visit, David asked repeatedly what time it was. Finally when I told him it was time to stop, with lightning speed he climbed onto a chair he had previously positioned for that purpose, grabbed the gun, and shot me again!

The visit after that, the gun was gone from the playroom. But curiously, David's aggression decreased markedly. He was afraid of his own aggression and he wanted me to be strong enough to stop him. That was his silent message.

When six-year-old Johnny came for his weekly play therapy session, the whole office would batten down the hatches and prepare for a state of siege. He was like quicksilver and felt that the whole building was his terrain. He was a match for Houdini in disappearances, and one time he was found hiding behind the furnace in the basement. Johnny was accident-prone as well as deaf, had been in and out of hospitals with various contusions, abrasions, and broken bones, and he appeared to have absolutely no fears at all. Yet he had terrible nightmares, and would awaken screaming in the night. In the playroom, where he had the security of confinement and limits, he was an absolute joy. In many ways he reminded me of my youngest son Mark at about age three—the engaging grin, the hint of the devil in his eye, the creative imagination. And I had retrieved Mark from the roof of the house once, I recalled. I thanked Mark silently now for helping prepare me to cope with Johnny. Mark had made it; Johnny will make it too—if we can just keep him alive.

However victimized Johnny may have been in other settings, he was always the rescuer in the playroom. His play was transparently symbolic, right out of therapy textbooks. He pantomimed many of his traumatic experiences, always casting himself in the role of rescuer. He was the heroic fireman who braved the flames to save the child. He was the tender doctor, gravely concerned with the battered child, gently solicitous with me, the distraught "mother." He always accepted my "Oh thank you doctor (fireman, ambulance driver, policeman) for saving my child!" with a studied nonchalance that would have drawn "bravos" on the stage. He told me what went on at home by manipulating the dolls in the dollhouse. His school problems were graphically illustrated with the dolls in the toy schoolhouse. His fantasies were very explicit. The little boy doll would climb up on the roof of the house and fall down the chimney, or would run away and be brought home by the toy cops. Big sister doll was always poking her nose in other peoples' business.

And Papa doll went to bed on top of Mama doll.

"Oh," I signed brightly in a rather futile attempt at interpretation. "Papa loves Mama."

Johnny looked at me with scorn. "That's not Papa!" he signed. "That's me!"

"Oh," I signed with cheeriness. "That's you!"

He moved in for the kill. Triumphantly, and with a devilish twinkle in his eye, he pointed to the supine female doll. "That's not Mama," he signed, "that's you!"

Gee, Coach, what do I do now? "Oh," I signed weakly. "That's me."

Dear Johnny, I thought, wherever you are now; keep your ebullient sense of fun. But remember our "mini-workshop" and take those limits with you out into the big wide hazardous world. With all its sham, drudgery, and broken dreams, I thought, remembering my own desiderata, it's still a beautiful world. I want the life you save to be your own.

I thought of the other children, and how the significant moments came when something happened to make us feel really close. When Bobby and I shook hands; when Carrie shared her feelings of rejection; when I had revved up my motor and entered Bruce's closed circle; when I had told David it was okay not to like me but he couldn't try to hurt me. I wanted to rewrite that talk to the parents: give your deaf child permission to be close. Share your world with him and he will come to you. He really needs you, you know.

....

As I put the notes away I found my memories moving to my own grand-children. Denny's oldest boy had been two and a half the last time I saw him, and he remembered the signs we had used the summer before. Signs made sense to Jackson, even though he wasn't deaf. He and Grandma Holly started on "Row, Row, Row Your Boat" and graduated to "more milk, please." "Funny Grandma Holly," he said to his dad. Baby brother Travis was too young to sign, but he loved to be rocked, and I rocked and rocked as I pulled from my memory all the rockabye songs my own mother had sung two generations ago. "Johnny sees her, ha, ha, ha/ Now I'll catch you, tra la la/ Nay, nay, nay/ Go a-way/ I'll not dance with you today."

Later, if Travis wanted to, we would sing the songs together in signs. If Jackson was any indication, he would probably want to.

sixteen

Man Also Needs to Attain
His Goals

The last entries in my folder were year-old press clippings. On a bright spring day, I opened the morning paper, as was my habit with my breakfast coffee. I had long since given up trying to lip read the TV news broadcasters. And my fears were realized. The Senate had failed to override the President's veto of the Rehabilitation Act. The administration called the Act a "budget buster," and viewed it as a test case; the press interpreted the failure to override as a "clear signal" that the public wanted to cut down on the "inflationary aspects of federal spending."

On the same front page I had noted that President Nixon had assured South Vietnam's President Nguyen Van Thieu that he would ask Congress for funds "sufficient to assure essential economic stability and rehabilitation" for South Vietnam as it "moves from war to peace."

God knew that I was thankful that the Vietnam War was over, and I couldn't really fault the President's wish to "assure stability" for South Vietnam, particularly since one of the cardinal lessons of the playroom was "what we have messed up we can put back together again."

But hadn't the President gotten his rehabilitation priorities mixed up? In my fantasy I switched the priorities and rewrote the news articles in my mind.

....

"Yesterday Congress failed to override the President's veto of the Rehabilitation Act for South Vietnam. The Act was called a 'budget buster'. The administration viewed it as a test case; the press interpreted the failure to override as a 'clear signal' that the public wanted to cut down on the 'inflationary aspects of defense spending.'"

On the same front page, (my fantasy continued), "President Nixon has assured the physically disabled of America that he would ask Congress for funds 'sufficient to assure the essential economic stability and rehabilitation' of handicapped people as they move to take their rightful places as contributing members of American society."

No way.

My concern was personal as well as professional. I had been a rehabilitation client and now I was attempting to rehabilitate emotionally disturbed deaf people. The clinic was funded by the Federal Rehabilitation Act. Did our work represent the "inflationary aspects of public spending?" If we didn't do it, who would? Were mental health services for the deaf becoming a luxury the United States could no longer afford?

What do you do, I wondered, to preserve essential services for the deaf that are already guaranteed for the hearing? Mount a forum? Become politically strident? Persuade the states to assume the fiscal responsibility when the existing state mental health programs were being cut back? Send the parents to their local community mental health centers for therapy without sign language?

Ultimately, in response to public pressure, the Rehabilitation Act was modified and some of the cuts were restored. But our own five year grant was terminated at the end of the first grant year. Now, with a reduced staff, we were struggling to stay alive, while the demand for our services continued to grow. Trained in mental health, we were learning to become political advocates on behalf of our deaf clients.

So Sisyphus had reached the brow of that hill and the gods had rolled the stone back down to the bottom again. Man finds his salvation in the struggle, but man needs to attain his goals, I thought. Could we mobilize sufficient "faith in the process of life" to start the long road up again?

seventeen
I'm Doing It My Way Now

I leaned back in my chair. What's the feeling, Holly? Where are you now?

The folder was on the desk in front of me, closed. I have finished my training, I thought. This folder's pretty full. I should retire it. Label it "Apprenticeship" and start a new one, labeled "Career." I placed it in the back of my bottom drawer, and mused again: What was I feeling now?

One feeling was satisfaction; I had gone to a conference at the Youth Authority Reception Center and they had found a sign language volunteer to visit Joe every day to talk with him and interpret for him. They had scheduled neurological and audiological examinations, and soon he would be wearing hearing aids for the first time. He would be on probation, and they were placing him in a vocational training center where there were a couple of other deaf kids who signed.

I had also been to a conference at the residential psychiatric treatment center where eight-year-old Joe had been placed. He saw my car coming up the drive and raced out to meet me.

"Bridge you!" he signed in excitement.

"Yes," I signed back. "Today I came across the bridge to see you!"

"Bridge me! Play, play, play! Please, please, ask, ask, ask!"

"No," I replied, my heart turning over. "I can't take you with me across the bridge to the playroom. But I hope I can come and see you again soon."

His right fist struck his palm and came forward with a sweeping motion. "Next week, Monday?"

The treatment staff was learning sign language too, and investigating the nearby total communication school for Joe.

But the feeling was frustration, too. The clinic had moved from "abrupt termination" to "orderly phase-out," but all that bought was a little more time. Time was a valuable commodity and one that was incessantly in short supply as the search for financial support constantly interfered with the time needed to see patients. But we were not alone in our quest, and this gave us a strong feeling of community.

I found myself reflecting on Mary's visit again. "We are all different, Mary," I said to her, "old and young, male and female, deaf and hearing, black and white, and with varying degrees of health, wealth, and wisdom. But underneath the differences we all belong to the same community of human beings, with the same needs to love and be loved."

Learning to love yourself is not easy. My own journey showed me that. Maybe the first step is getting permission to be close. I thought of Jim, pushing his stone up his mountain. "It's okay now, Jim," I said softly. "The way down is the way up." Maybe that is what therapists are for, to help us set our sights on that mountain top again—to give us permission to be close.

A few nights ago I met another deaf man at a party. After watching me sign for a few moments, he said: "You're like my wife; you came late to sign language. Were you 'oral' a long time like she was?"

"Yes," I replied. "I 'passed' a lot too, because my speech was good. I pretended. But it's a lot more comfortable now, because I don't have to pretend any more."

That night I had a vivid dream. I dreamed that Father was preaching from the pulpit in sign language, and I felt the old anxiety rising. I stood in my pew and found myself walking slowly down the aisle. I felt, with terrible intensity, that I must communicate with him, but he continued to preach as if I was not there, standing in front of him. I tried to speak, but the words would not come. Finally Father stopped preaching and looked down at me.

"Yes, Holly?" he said.

"I can't say it, Father," I whispered. "You sign too fast for me."

Father drew down his heavy brows in a disapproving frown. "The words, Holly," he said. "Get the words. You're old enough to understand them now."

I woke with a start. But Father didn't know signs. My God, I thought in a sudden flash of insight, am I playing that game in sign language? Is that why I block? I wanted to get in touch with the feeling of the dream. The Voice of Authority. I block when I try to relate to the Voice of Authority. "Try hard, Holly." And the Voice of Authority also includes, especially includes, someone who signs better than I. This does not happen in the patient-therapist relationship because there is no Voice of Authority. This does not happen when I am giving a talk in sign language, because I am the Voice of Authority. Then I have something important to say, too.

This is important business, I thought, as I closed my eyes and pictured an ending to the dream. Maybe this is what my walk down memory lane has led me to. I walked firmly up the chancel steps and faced Father in the pulpit. He stood only about three inches above me, and I held his gaze. I put my hands on his shoulders. "It's okay, Father. It's okay to be close. I understand now. I'm not a Victim any more."

Sleep was gone, so I got out of bed and pulled on my robe. While I was warming milk on the kitchen stove, I recalled a recent experience and wondered how it tied into the dream. I woke on May 7, my thirtieth wedding anniversary, and said, "Oh, the hell with it. I will call in sick." As I lifted the phone to dial, the voices in my head said faintly, "Have you been a good girl, Jane?" But another voice overrode them. "Look, Mom and Dad, I'm doing it my way now."

I spent the day walking in the park, admiring the rhododendrons and talking to the squirrels and blue jays. It was a marvelously emancipating experience. The next day (because I was so seldom ill) the staff solicitously asked after my health. "Oh, I wasn't sick. I just decided to spend the day in the park." A small thing, perhaps, but somehow I felt it was significant.

I picked up my cup of hot milk and walked over to my attic apartment window. Two years ago I had bought this old house, because it was high on a hill, and because it had been converted into five apartments. I was gradually filling it with tenants who sign.

Deaf or hearing—it didn't matter—as long as they were authentic human beings. (And there was someone who could answer the phone!)

As I looked out the window, I saw that the fog had not yet rolled in; the lights on the Bay Bridge were clear. I was forcibly struck anew that my journey had bought me to a view overlooking the place where my conscious memory began. Goat Island was hidden by the downtown high-rises, but I knew it was there, and sudden tears stung my eyes as the childhood memories flooded in. Why are you crying, Mommy? Do your legs hurt, too? My gaze slowly scanned the sleeping city below. Silence lay like a veil over the city; no strident sound of sirens, no squeal of tires, no crunch of metal on metal, no sound of footfalls on the pavement, no comforting call of foghorns, no cooing of doves in the back-yard dovecote, no sound of wind in the eaves, no party stereo through open windows, no barking dogs, no soft sounds of pleasure, no sudden cry of a sick child: but I knew they were all there. It was as if a light snowfall had buried the sounds of the city. It seemed to be waiting, caught in its stillness, and I realized that the only voice now in my head was Robert Frost's. I put down my cup and signed the words silently to myself: "The woods are lovely, dark and deep, but I have promises to keep...and miles to go before I sleep...and miles to go before I sleep."

eighteen

September 1998

Many years have passed since that night I scanned the city from my apartment window and finally felt that I could accept my past without regret, without resentment, and pursue my new journey with confidence and pride. I write now overlooking the Willamette River from the fourteenth floor of our retirement home, overlooking another city. I found that old manuscript when Laurel, my close friend and professional colleague, and I went through our papers, preparing to pull together our research data from the national study of adaptation to adult onset hearing loss we've been spending our time on. She and I are on "retirement recall" from the Langley Porter Psychiatric Institute, University of California, San Francisco.

How young that manuscript sounds to me now. Such a mixture of confidence, anxiety, stumbling insecurity, yet knowledge I was on the right track. And relief that I didn't have to pretend any more. I started writing it, I remember, when I offered some kind of writing sample to my Transactional Therapist, Duncan, and he surprised me with his praise. "Holly," he said, "you write well.

Keep at it. It's a wonderful form of self-psychotherapy." Emboldened, I had "kept at it." But as the years intervened, my life took such positive turns that I no longer needed to write about my own experiences. And not only my life, but also the lives of so many deaf people.

> ITEM
>
> The text telephone became widely used. Called a "TTY" after the first prototype, the Western Union Teletype that stood on the floor and resembled a small green roll top desk. But I could type-talk to anyone who had a similar model; an answering service soon sprang up to monitor calls from those who did not own a TTY; before long, the TTY became the TDD (telephone device for the deaf), a desk-top model with conversations printed on tape like that from an adding machine. When I called my kids, I didn't say, "we talked for an hour," I said, "we talked for three yards!" Every state now has a TDD relay system so I can call anywhere through it, and have the option of talking or typing. In many states the telephone company provides the instruments free to those who qualify. And more recently, e-mail bypasses even the relay systems.

> ITEM
>
> Research has identified American Sign Language as a language that stands by itself—not a signed representation of the English language. ASL has its own grammar and syntax and is used without voice. Voicing sign language is called "Signed English" or "Sign Supported Speech." The culturally deaf person must be bilingual, communicating in ASL and reading and writing in English.

> ITEM
>
> Deaf culture was strongly supported by the "Deaf President Now" protest at Gallaudet University in 1983. Deaf pride took a giant leap forward when I. King Jordan was named

President. The deaf (lower case) population—those whose first language is ASL-became a strong Deaf Culture. "Deaf" became a cultural description, not a disabiity. Those who become deaf later in life are usually referred to as "culturally hearing deaf" (lower case) persons who tend to use Signed English, if they sign at all. A smaller group of those who were born deaf (or who were deafened before language was established), and who depend on speech and speech reading, make up the population of "oral deaf" persons. And there are the audiologically deaf persons, a much larger population, especially the elderly, who can benefit from amplification.

ITEM

Support groups have grown rapidly. Self Help for Hard of Hearing People, Inc. (SHHH), with more than 16,000 members and chapters all over the country, and the national Association of Late Deafened Adults (ALDA) have had a remarkably positive impact on hard of hearing and culturally hearing deaf persons.

ITEM

Closed captioning has made television accessible to those hearing impaired people who have telecaption decoders attached to their TVs. The Americans with Disabilities Act requires that all new televisions be equipped with built-in decoders. Open captioning with stenotype or computer attachment to TV monitors, as well as voice-driven computer texts, are becoming helpful at meetings and conferences attended by hearing-impaired persons.

ITEM

The clinic did not terminate. It became part of the County Mental Health Program with continued affiliation with the University Department of Psychiatry.

ITEM

Cochlear implants have improved dramatically. Microtechnology enables even those with inner ear nerve deafness like mine to hear electronically.

ITEM

Deaf people trained as professional psychotherapists, of which I was one of the first, are now common. Today sign language interpreters are routinely added to clinical staff, computer-assisted notetaking transfers the spoken word into text. The problem now might only be: which sign language, Signed English or ASL?

....

My 'island of sound" has virtually disappeared now, but I was one of the first to receive a primitive cochlear implant. Yes, another run at being a guinea pig. I smile. Only four channels, and an unwieldy battery pack. I reach up and touch the base of my skull where the upgraded model now gives me sixteen channels. I could have another upgrade, but I don't want to risk another general anesthesia. It's like learning yet another new language; the modulations of the tones are nothing like the language I remember. I recall the time I visited my sister and her husband in North Carolina just after the first implant. He and I walked in the late afternoon across the fields beside their home, and I stopped suddenly. "What's that noise?" I asked, gripping his arm tightly. "I've never heard it before." He looked at me with awe and compassion. "It's crickets, Holly," he said. "Just crickets." And if I really want to be alone, I just pull the contact away from the magnet under my skin. Silence.

final words

Four years ago, twenty years after I immersed myself in "self-psychoanalysis," I traveled to Toronto to receive the I. King Jordan award for "outstanding achievement" from the Association of Late Deafened Adults. In my acceptance speech, I said:

"Like Sisyphus I have been climbing up the mountain, falling back, climbing up, falling back. But unlike Sisyphus, I have reached the top and look out on all the friendly ALDA faces I see in front of me. Thirty years ago, my pastor said to me: 'Holly, why don't you stop fighting the deafness and start using it?' If he were here today, I would say to him, 'See what you've done?'"

biographical note

Holly Elliott was familiar with forging new paths. To name only several: she was one of the first individuals with inner-ear nerve degeneration to receive a prototype cochlear implant and, several years later, was one of the first to have an implant upgraded. As she describes in this memoir, she was probably the first professionally trained deaf counselor-therapist. In her initial position as intern and then staff member at the University of California Center on Deafness, she became an advocate of *total communication*—a combination of sign language, lip-reading, and oral competency that was a new horizon for rehabilitation therapy for the deaf. Finally, in a more general sense of path-breaking, she made a courageous career shift at mid-life; after twenty-five years of marriage and child-rearing, she accepted her deafness and embarked on a retraining that eventuated in a distinguished professional career: a model that was unusual for women of her time, and still speaks to our twenty-first-century experience.

Holly was born in 1920, graduated with a BA in music from UCLA in

1941, married in 1944, and returned to college to study for an MA in rehabilitation counseling in 1968, receiving the degree in 1970. Thus she began her first professional position at age 50. After ten years' service at UCCD, she was asked to become director of an experimental five-year graduate program at San Francisco State University, training rehabilitation counselors to work with "minimal language-skilled deaf adults," that is, persons with no formal sign language and no formal schooling, most of whom were immigrants from Asia, South or Central America. Fifty of the fifty-two students trained in that program were still working in deaf rehabilitation ten years later. She returned to UCCD in 1985 to write and edit two books on Mental Health Assessment of Deaf Clients, one in 1987, the other in 1989. She finally retired from her association with the University of California in 1992.

Meanwhile, she was also active in the Methodist Church, being on the Board of Directors and President of the United Methodist Congress of the Deaf from 1982–88. She was instrumental in effecting the General Conference decision in 1992 to establish a National United Methodist Committee on Developing Deaf Ministries. The Committee has now become a funded and staffed National United Methodist Committee on Ministries with Deaf, Late-Deafened, Hard of Hearing, and Deaf-Blind People.

Holly continued her work after retirement by collaborating with her close friend, Dr. Laurel Glass, on a federally funded project dealing with adult onset hearing loss, moving with Laurel to Portland, Oregon, in 1996. In the spring of 2000, however, just a few months after her 80th birthday, a massive stroke permanently paralyzed her left side, and she died on October 19th, 2002.

—Jay Elliott

Printed in the United States
205682BV00001B/151-231/P

9 781935 052081